I0491933

This Book Belongs To:

fullweb-publishing.co.uk

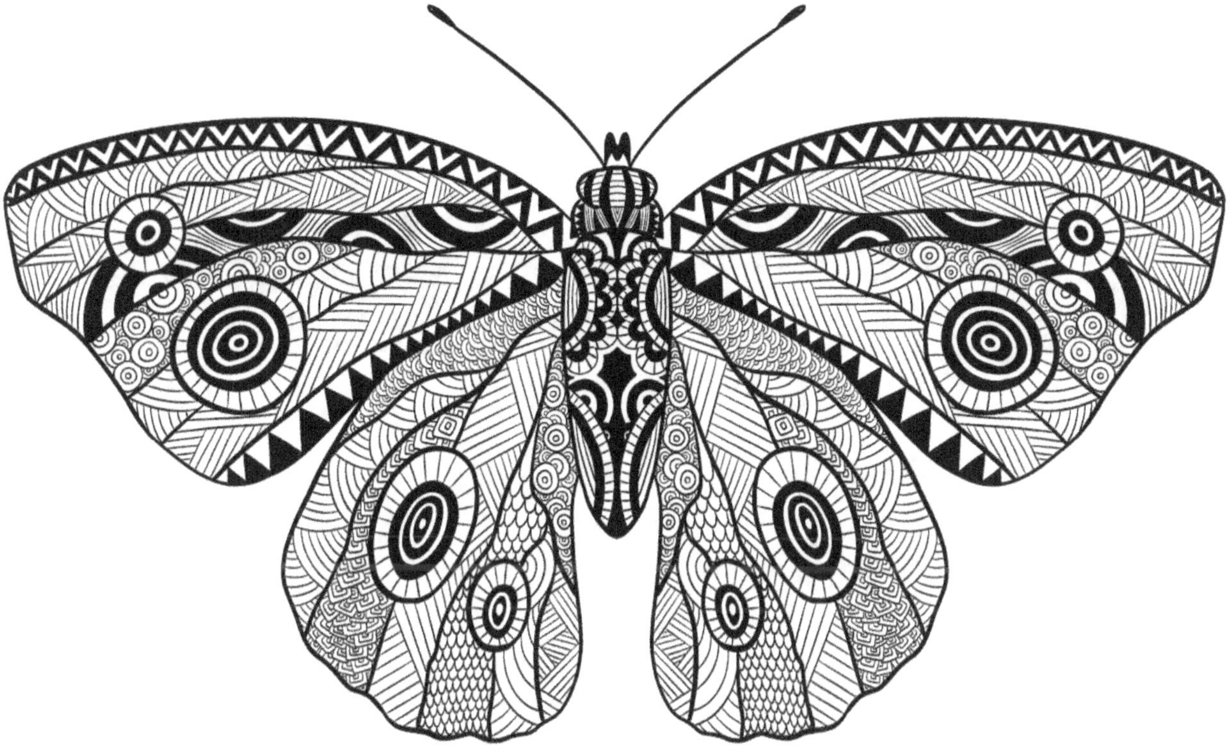

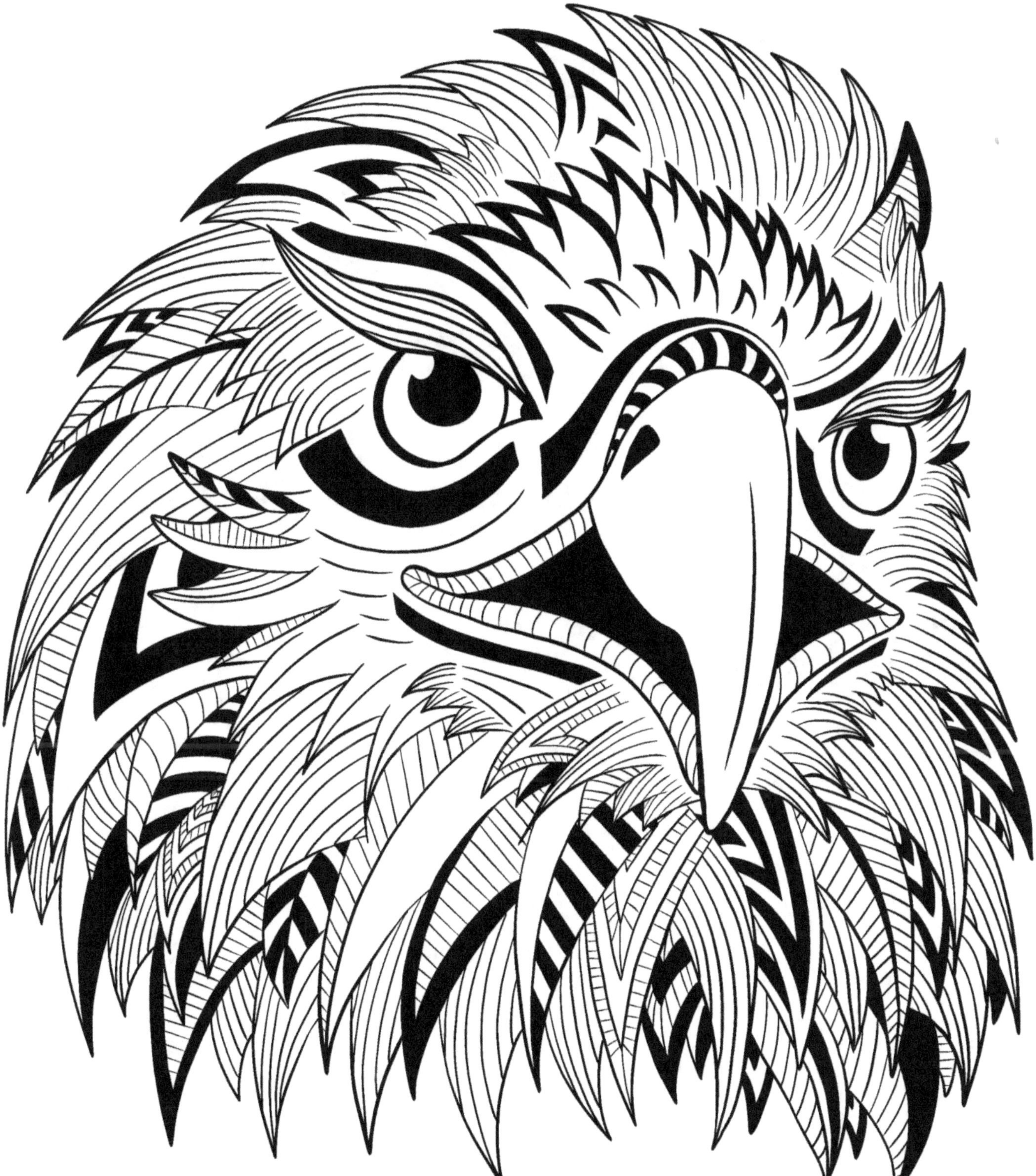

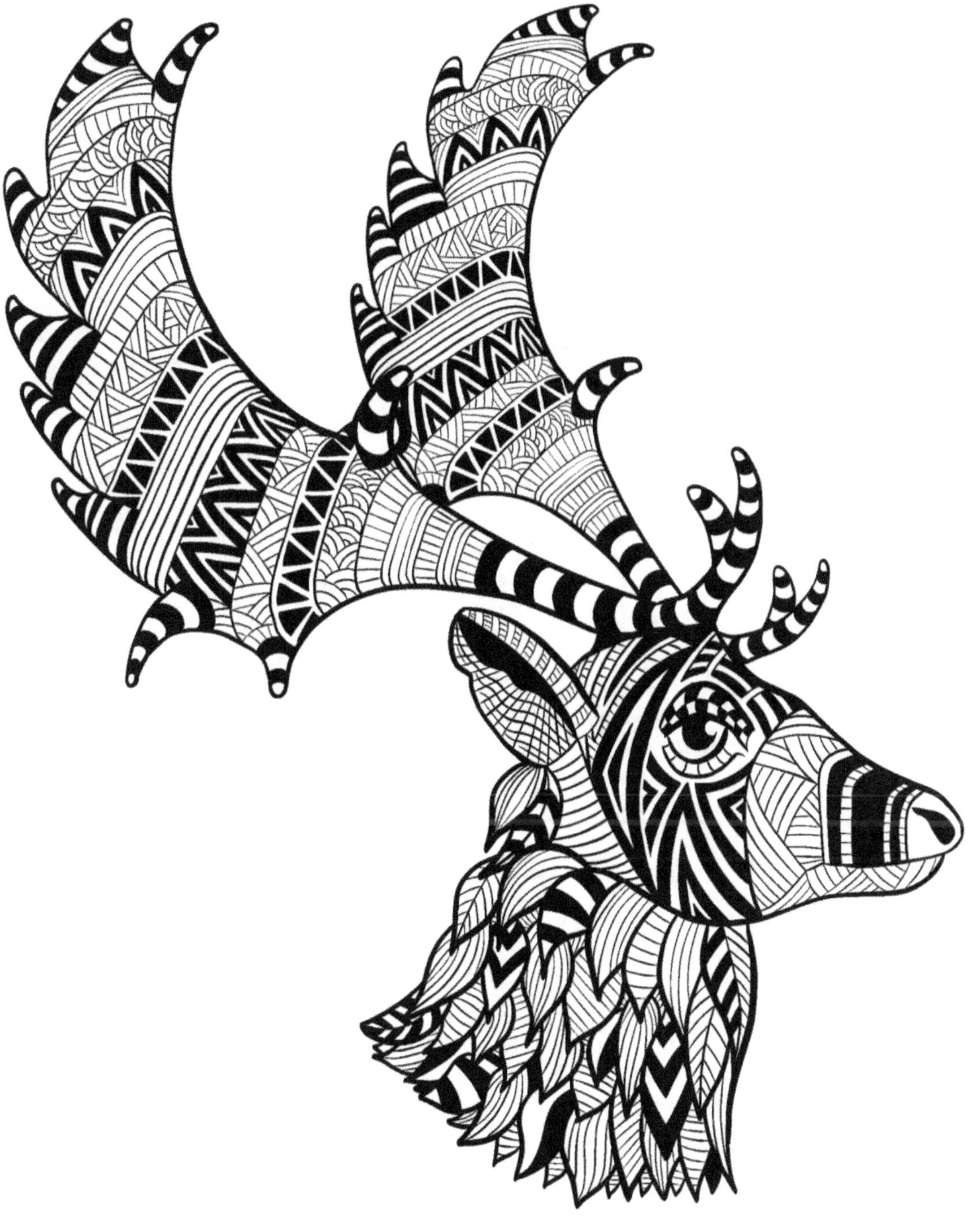

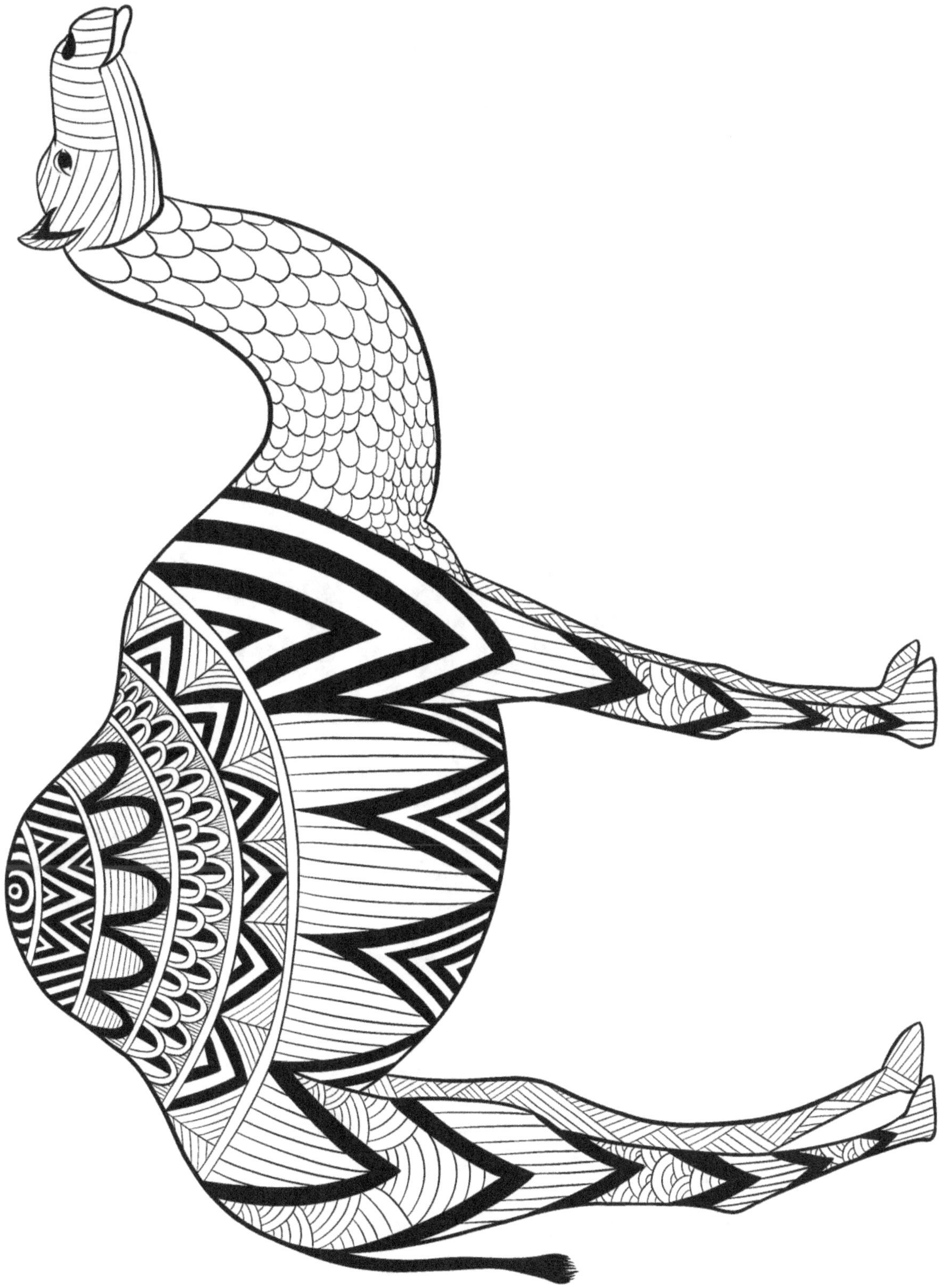

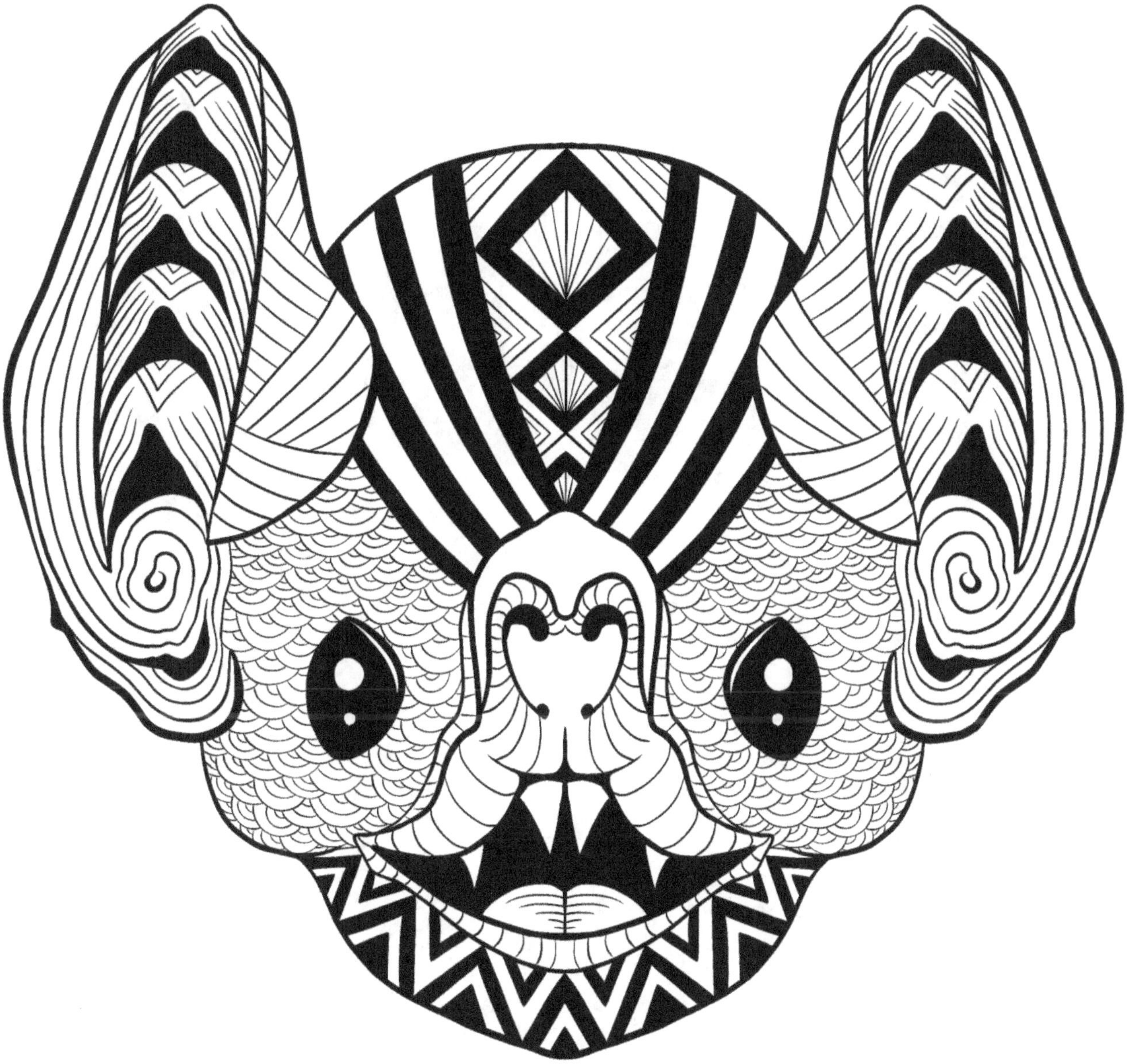

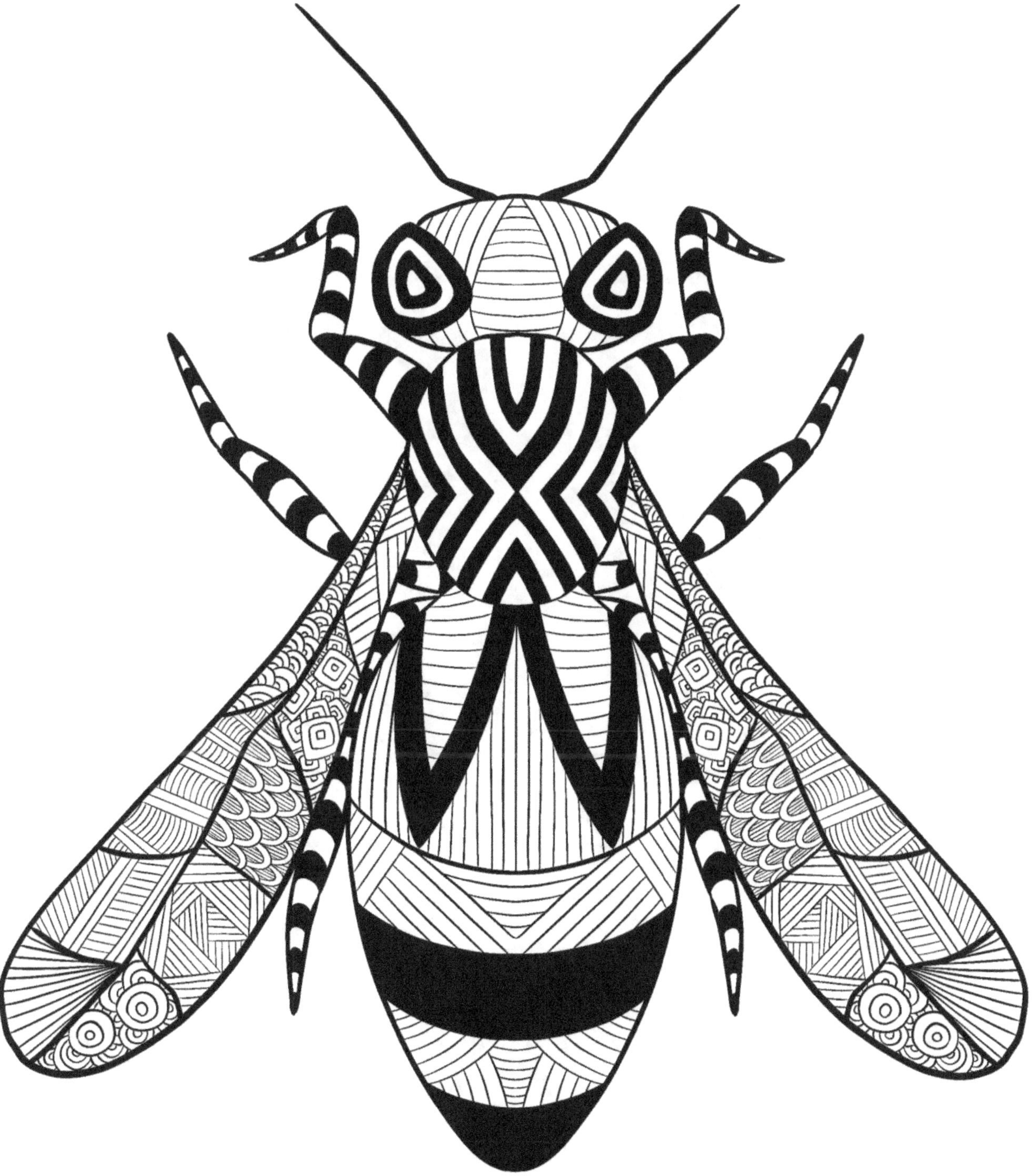

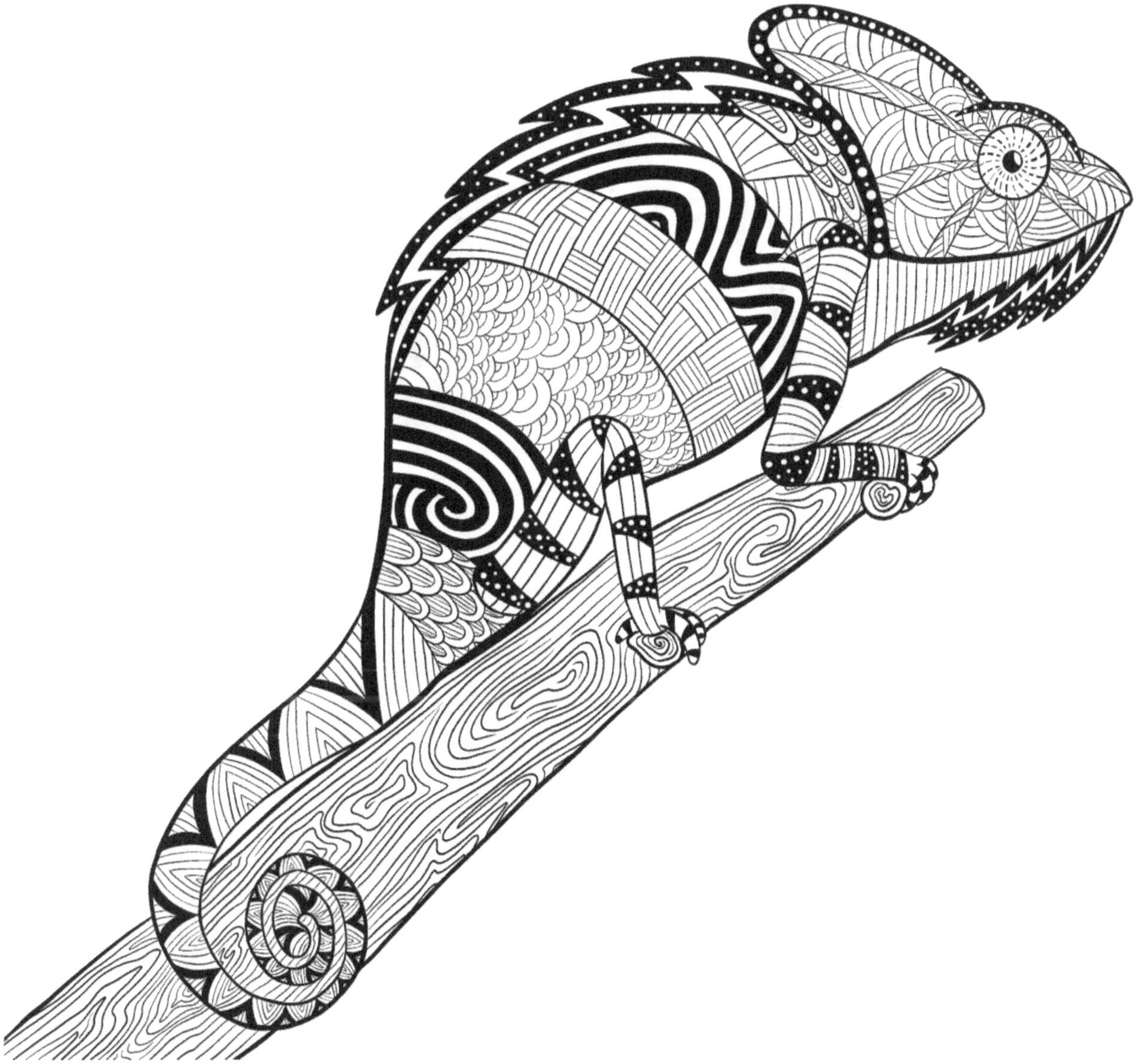

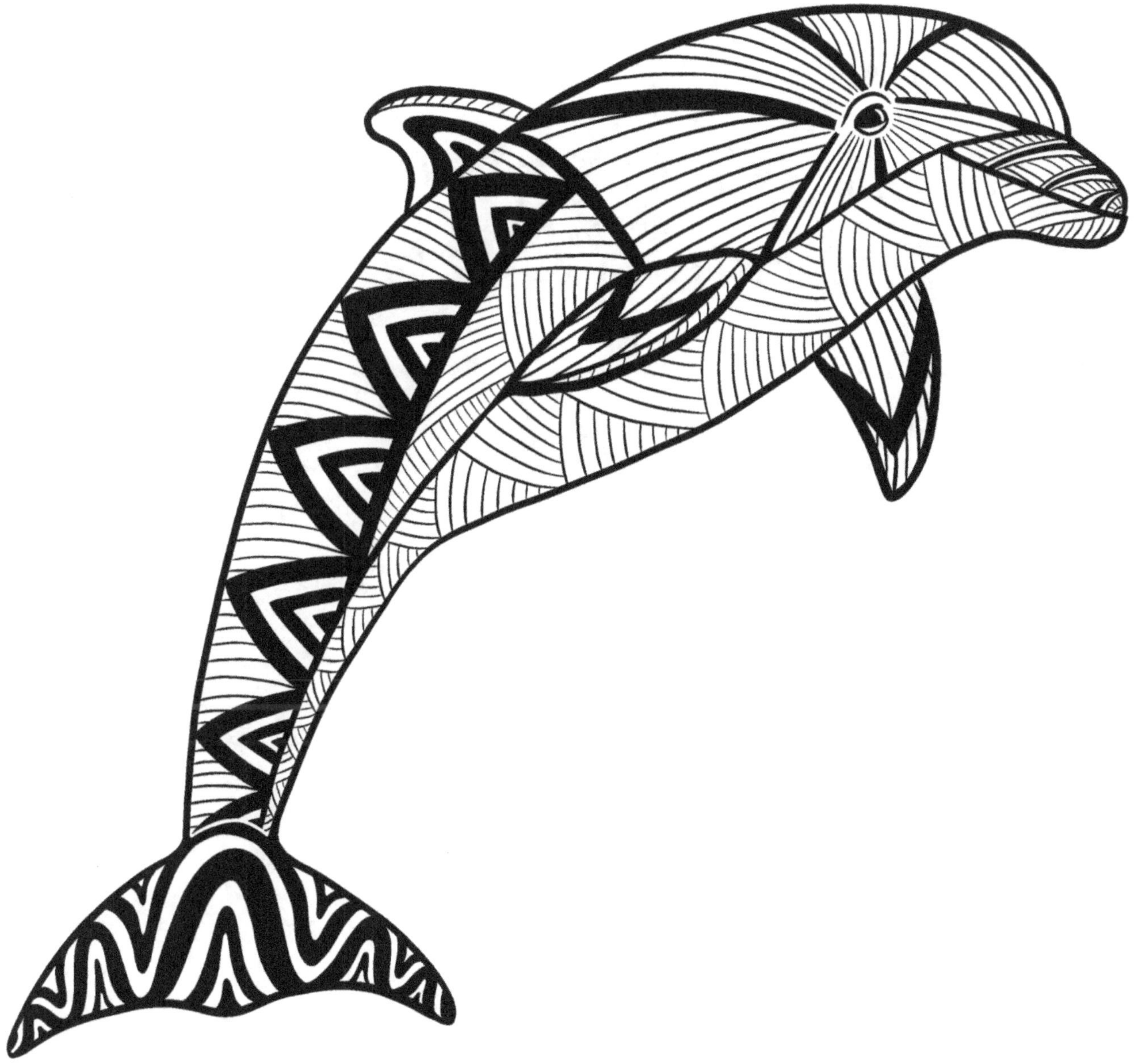

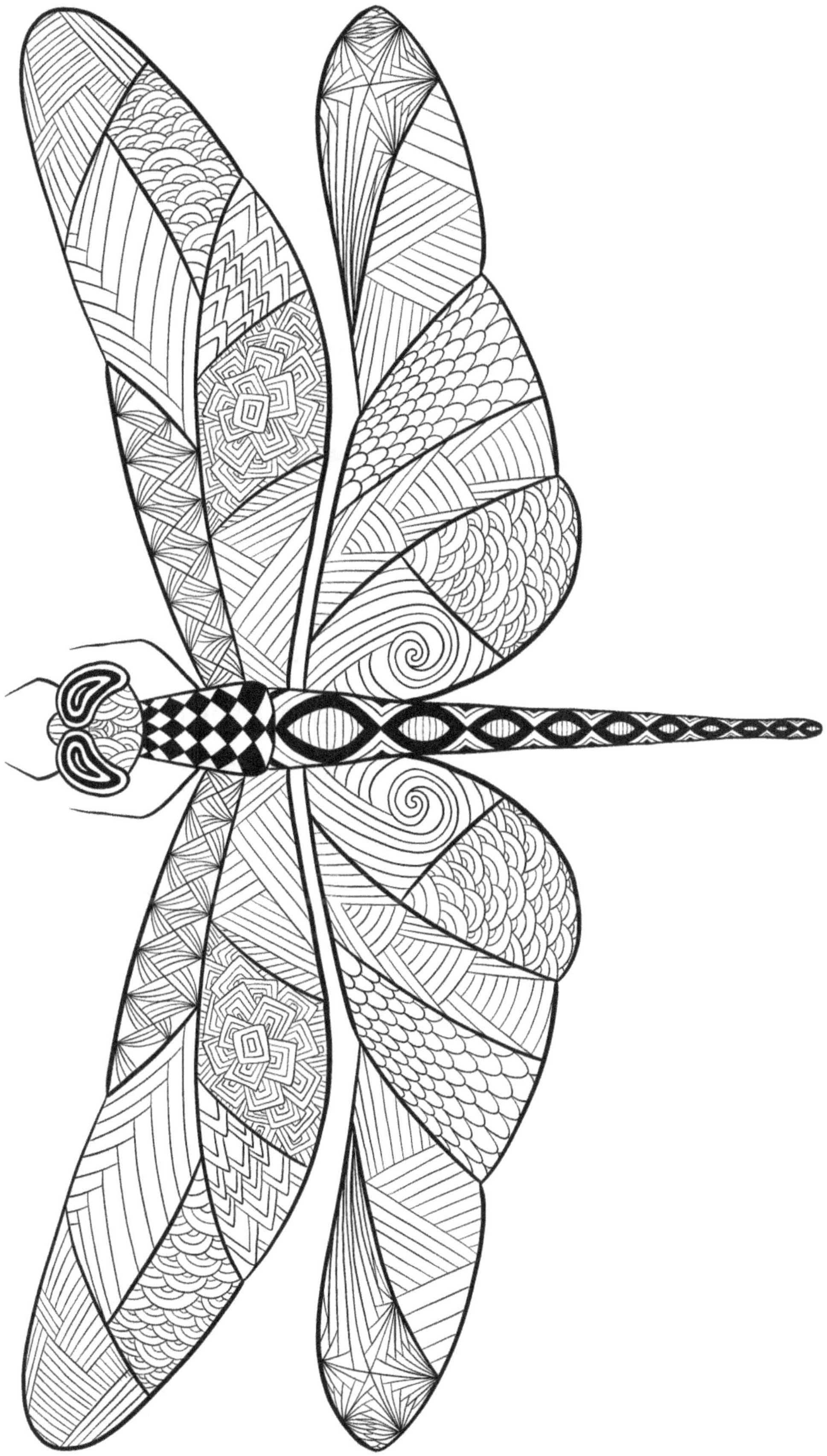

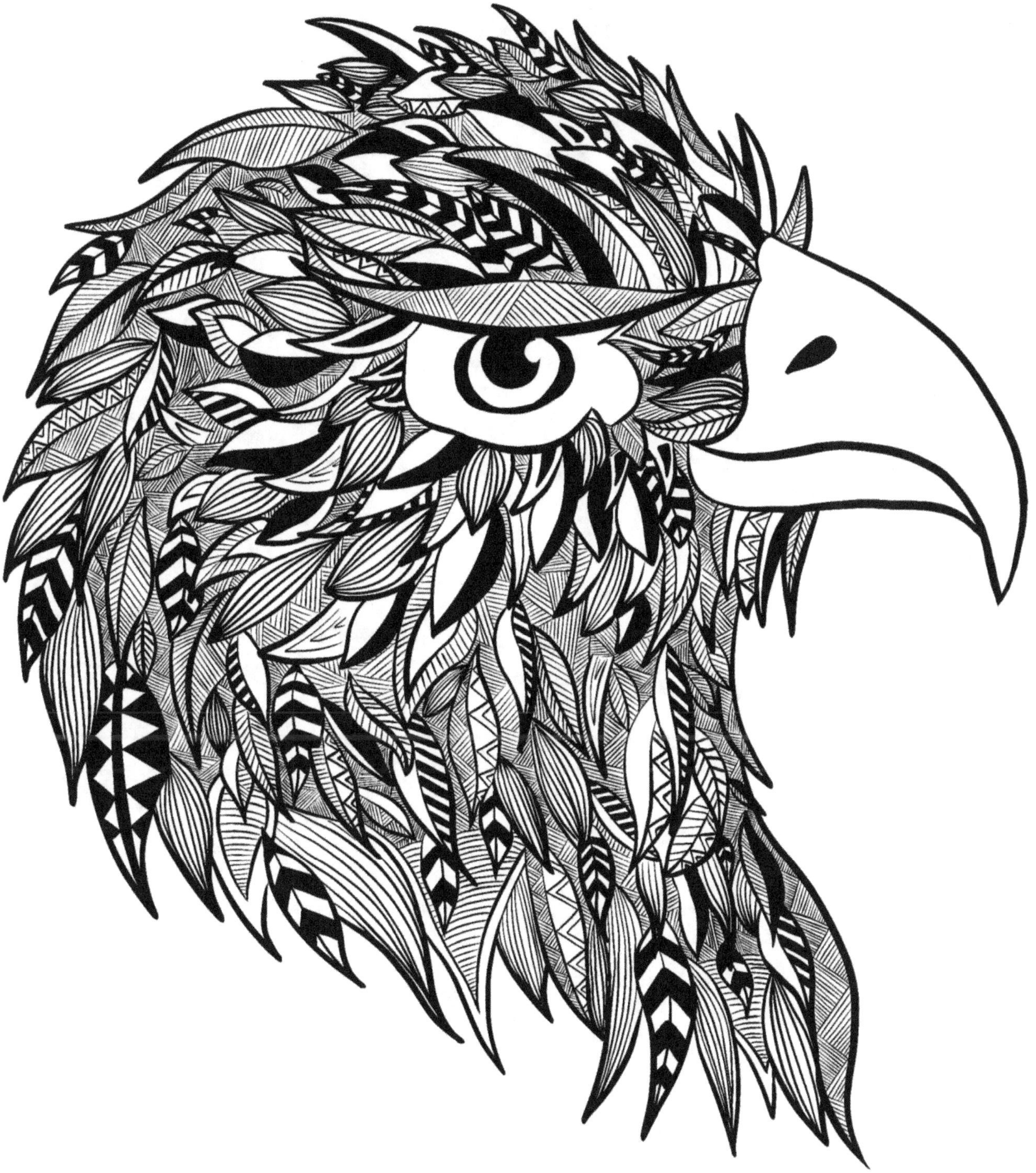

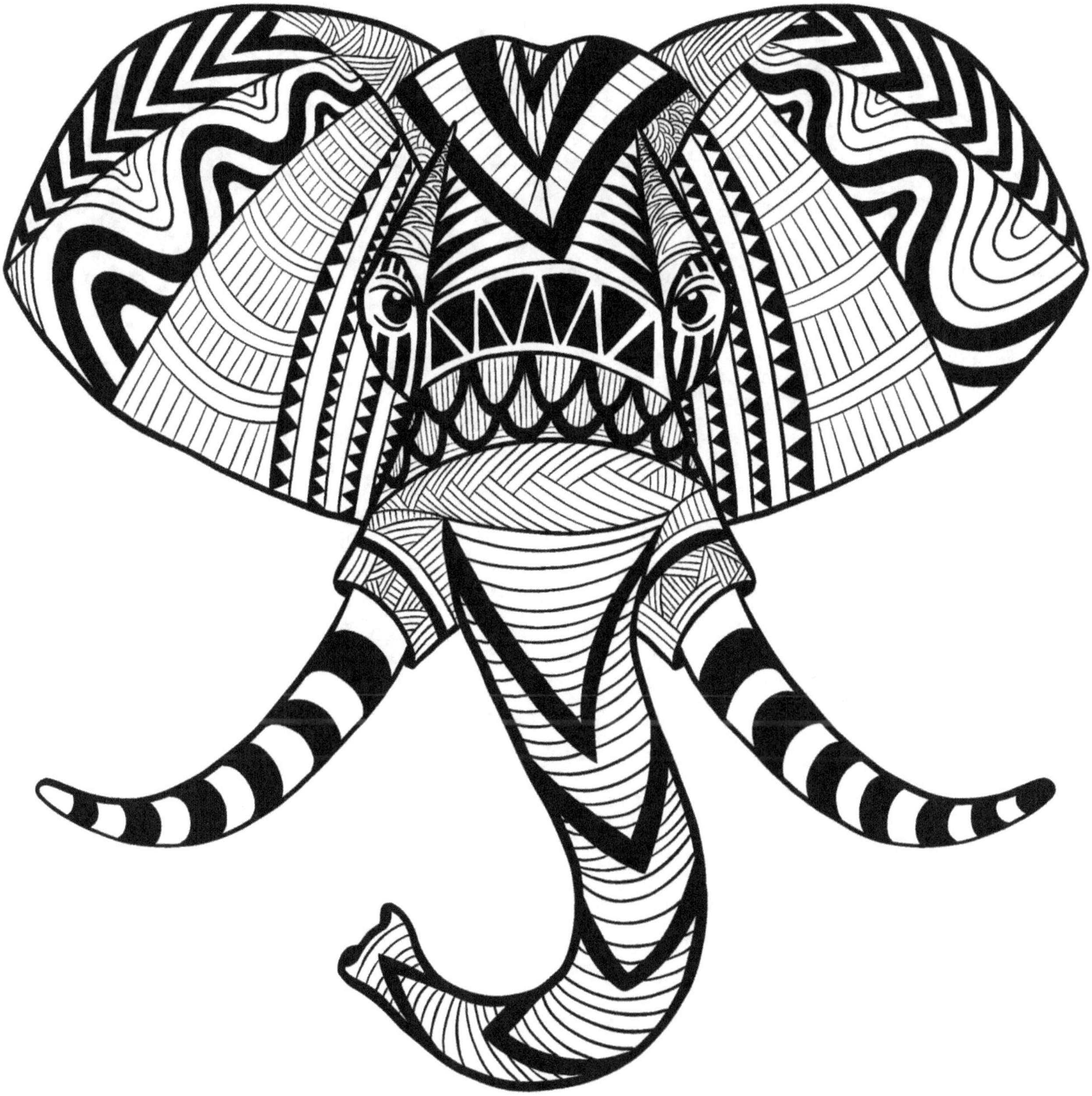

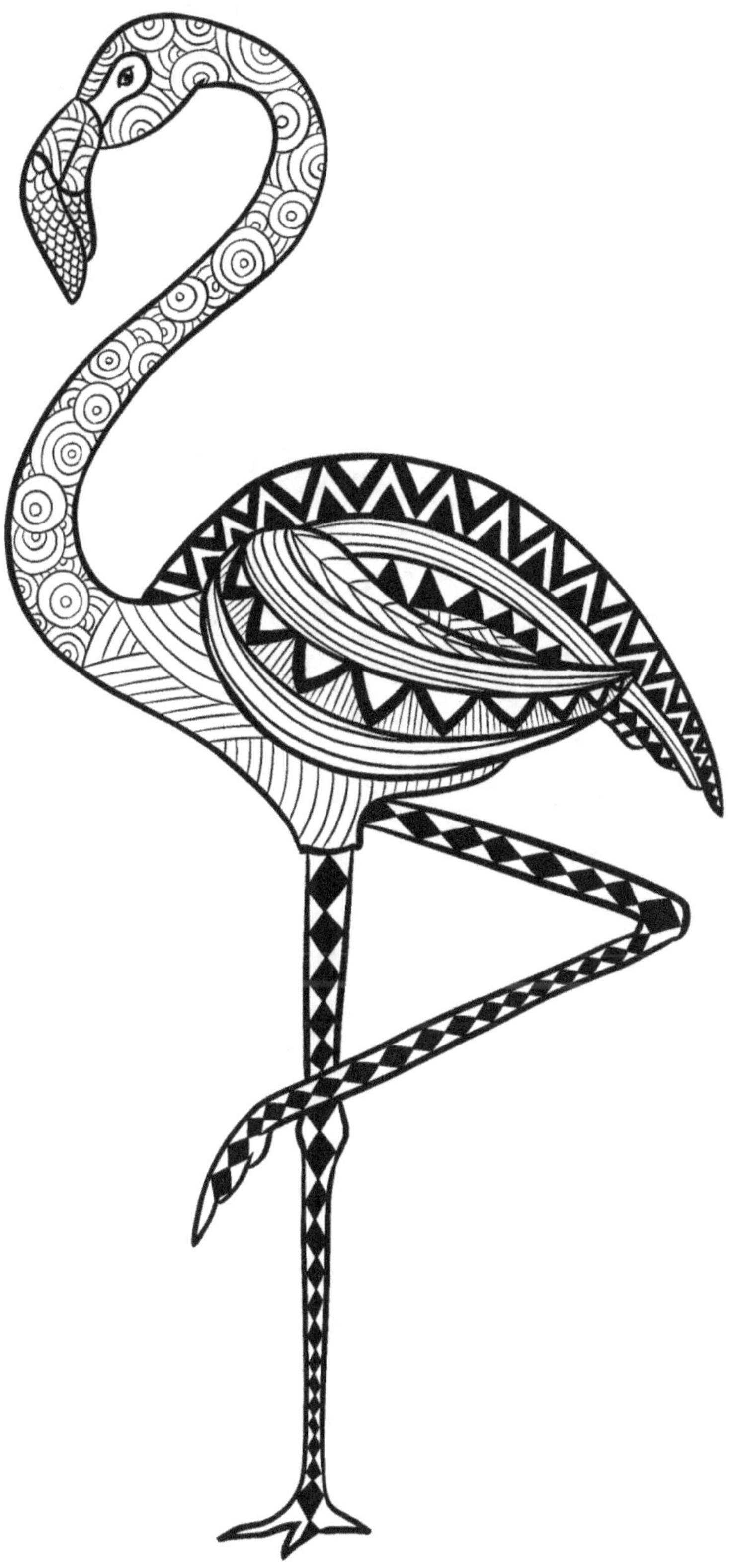

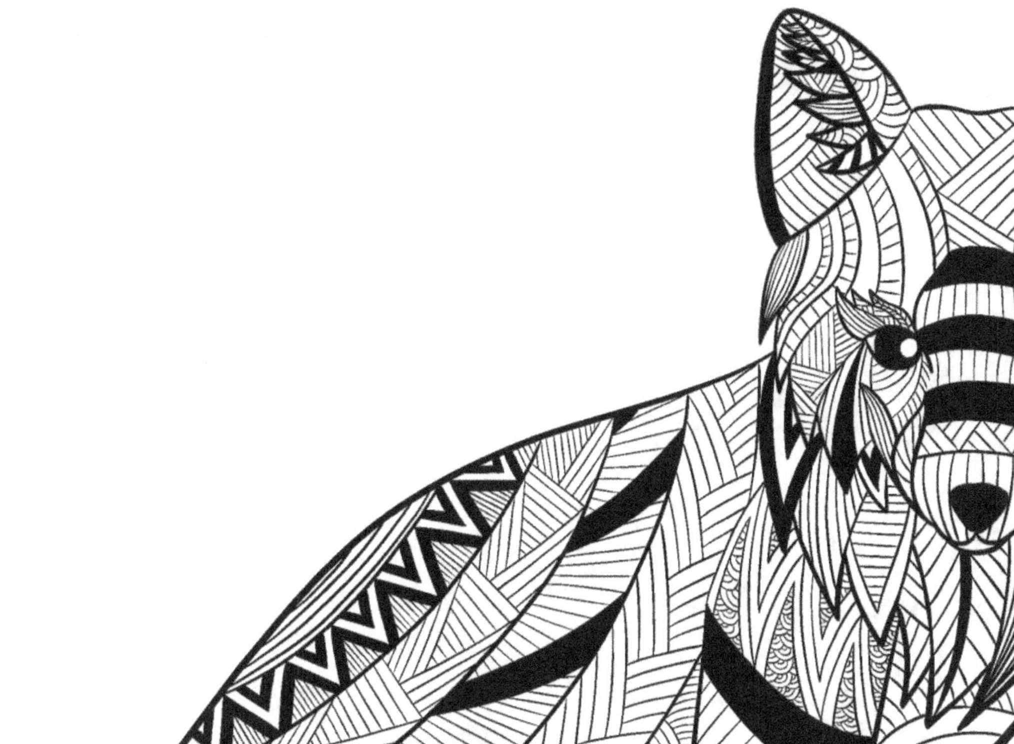

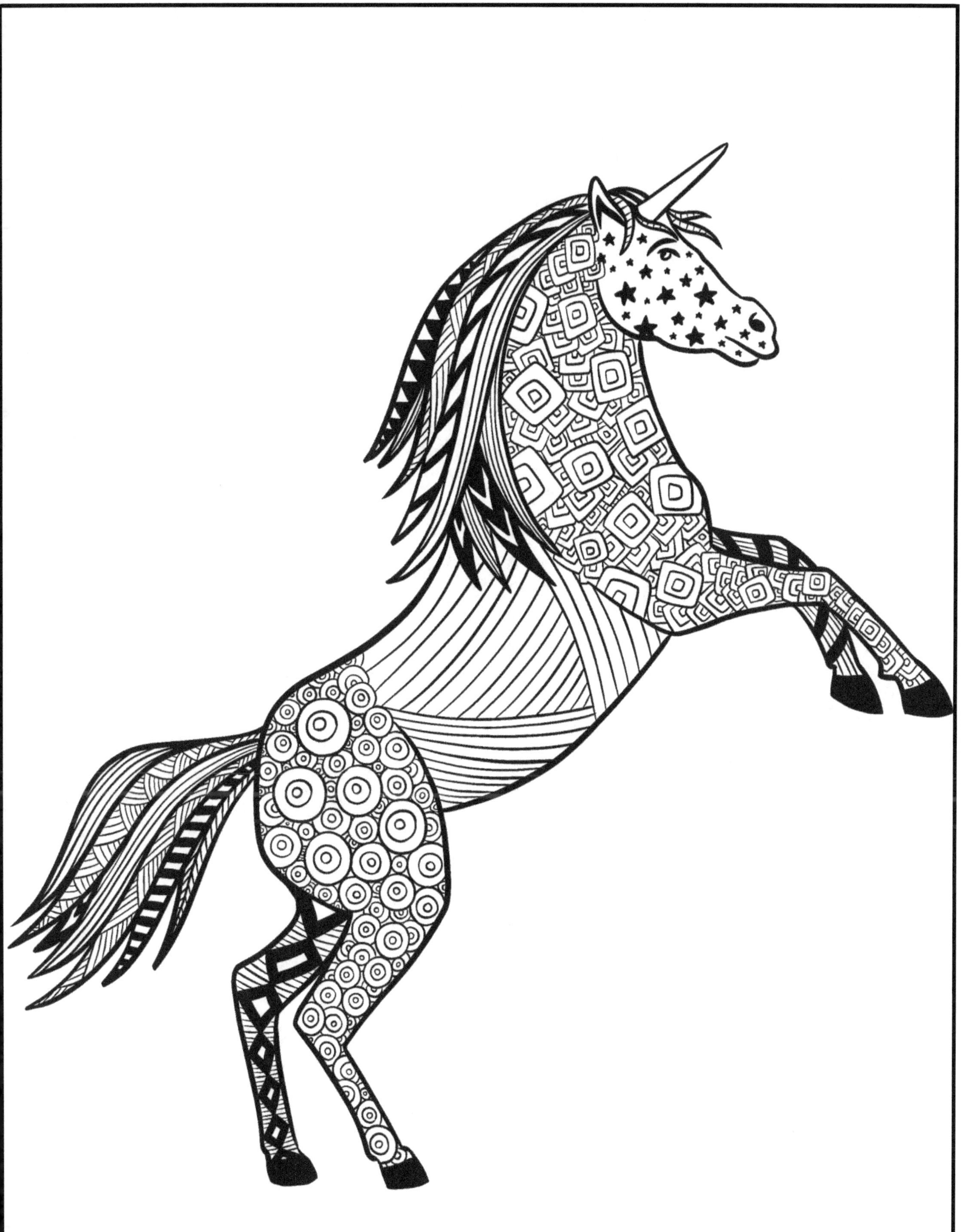

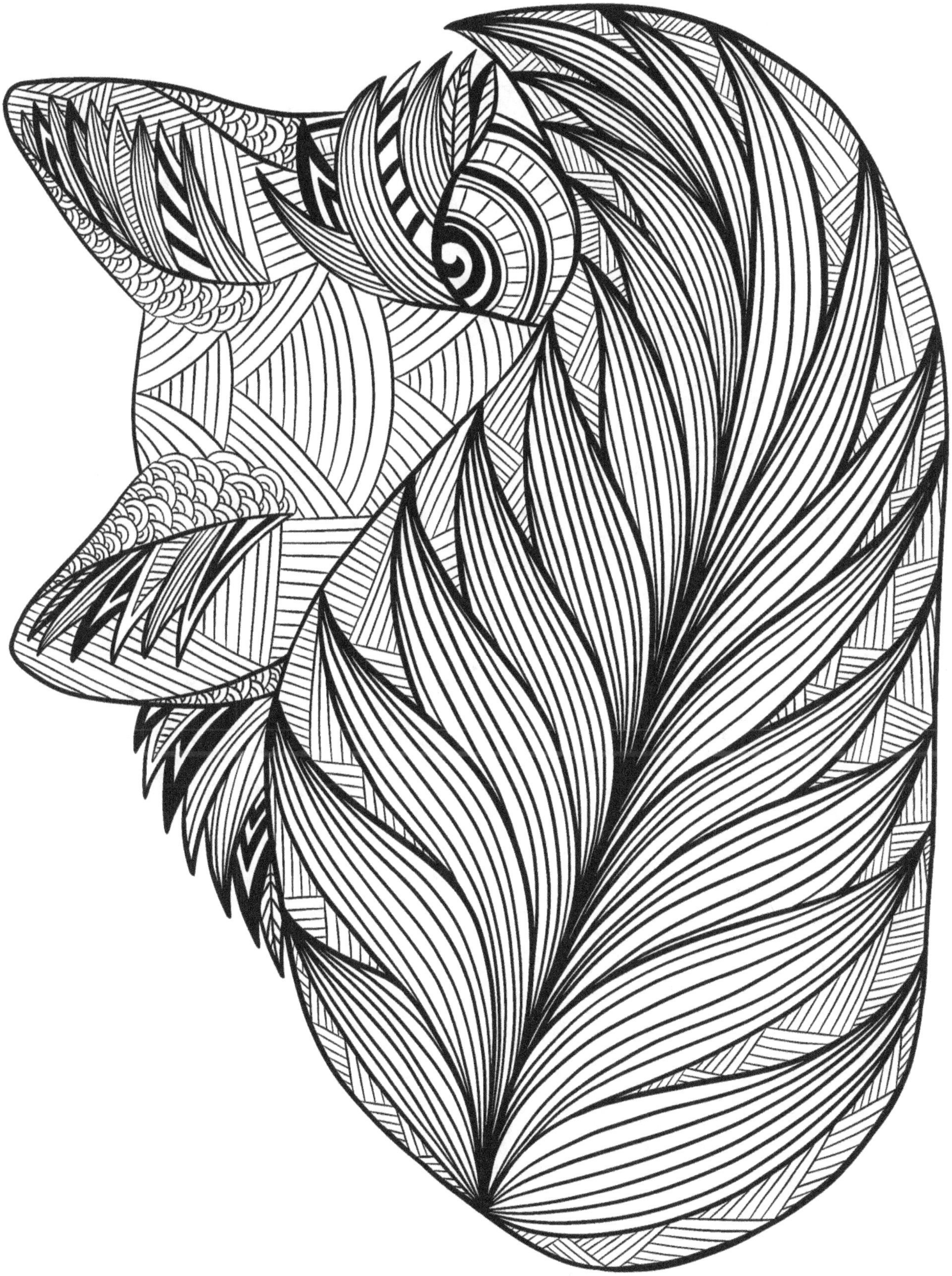

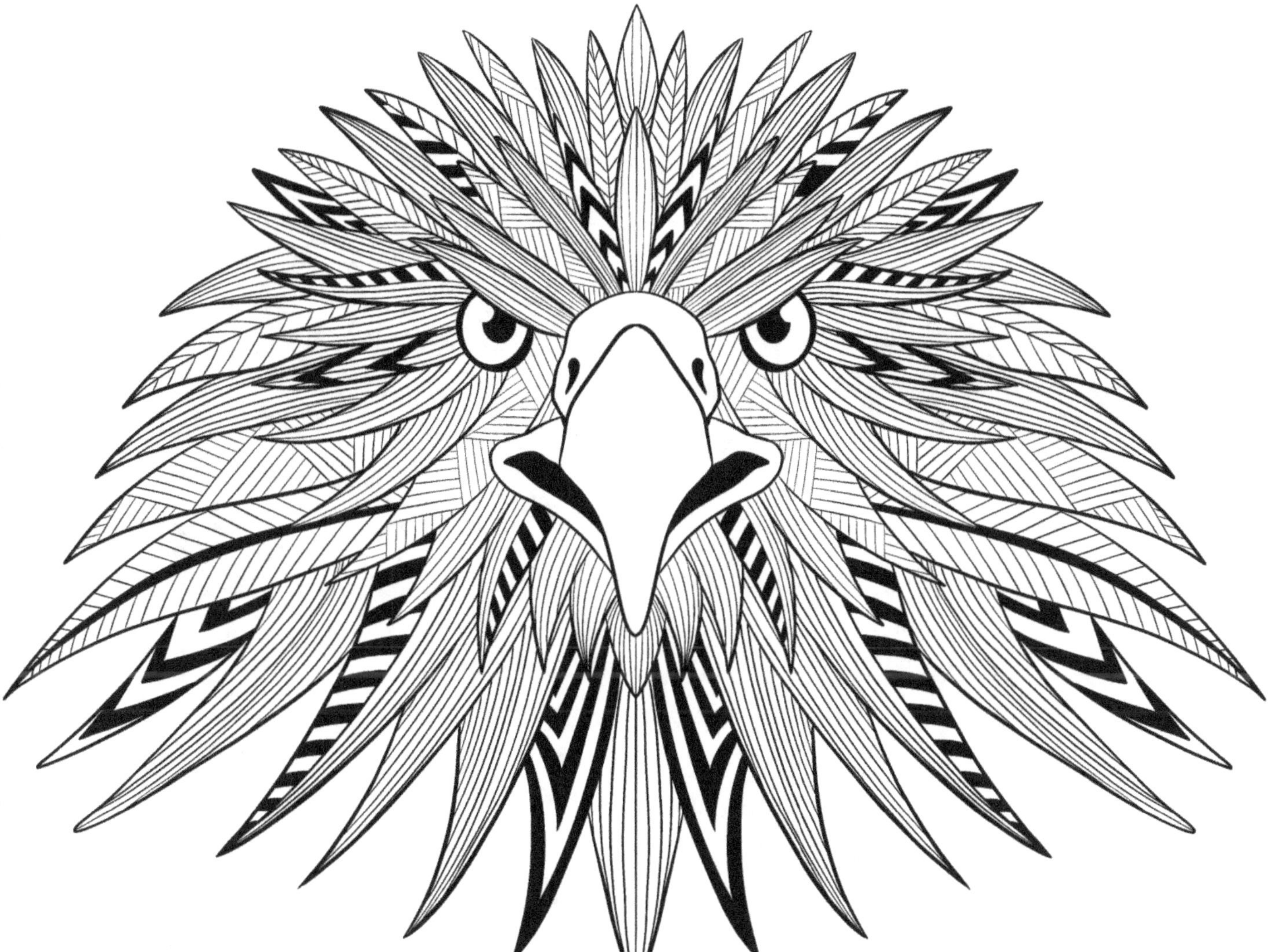

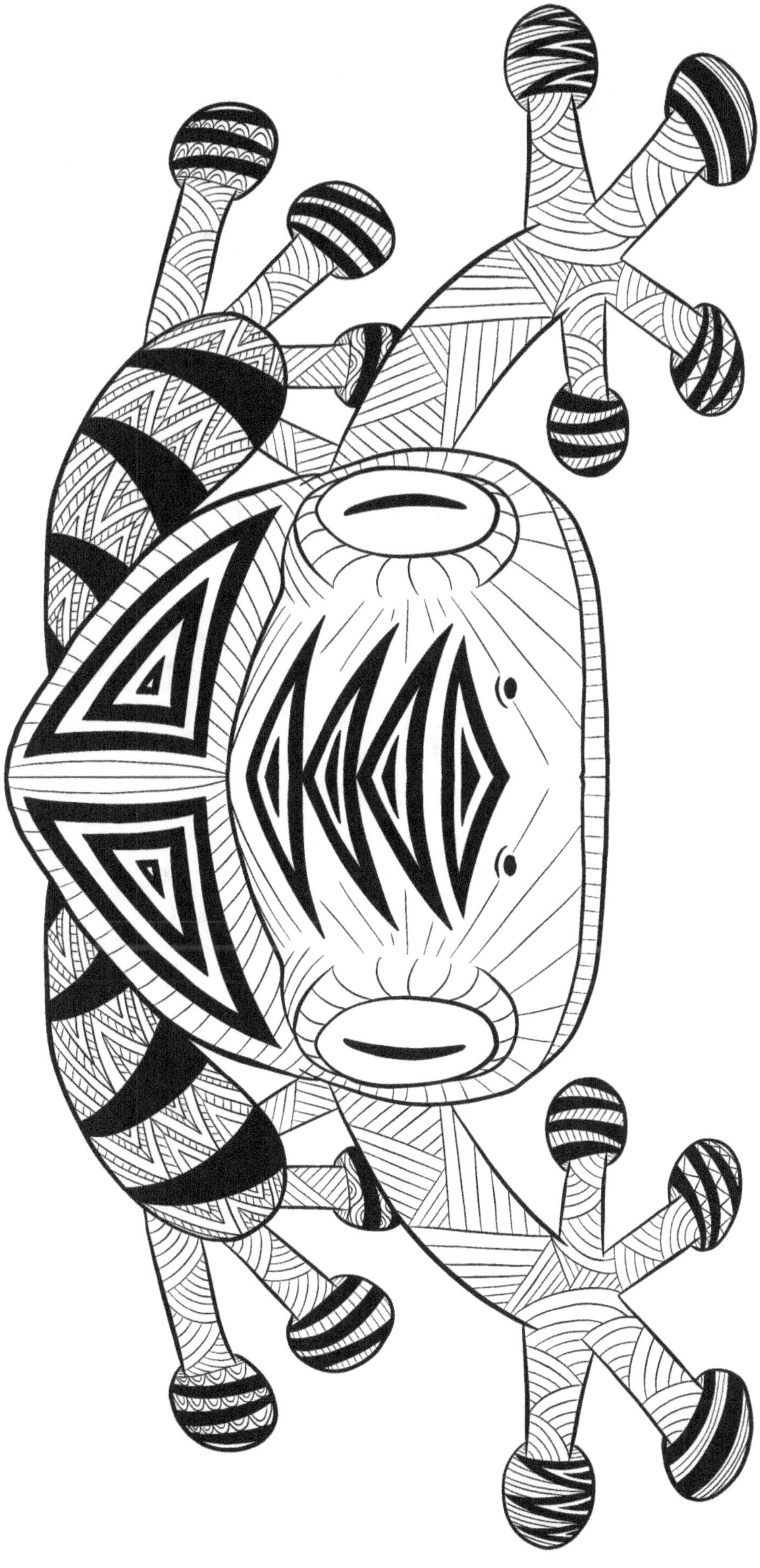

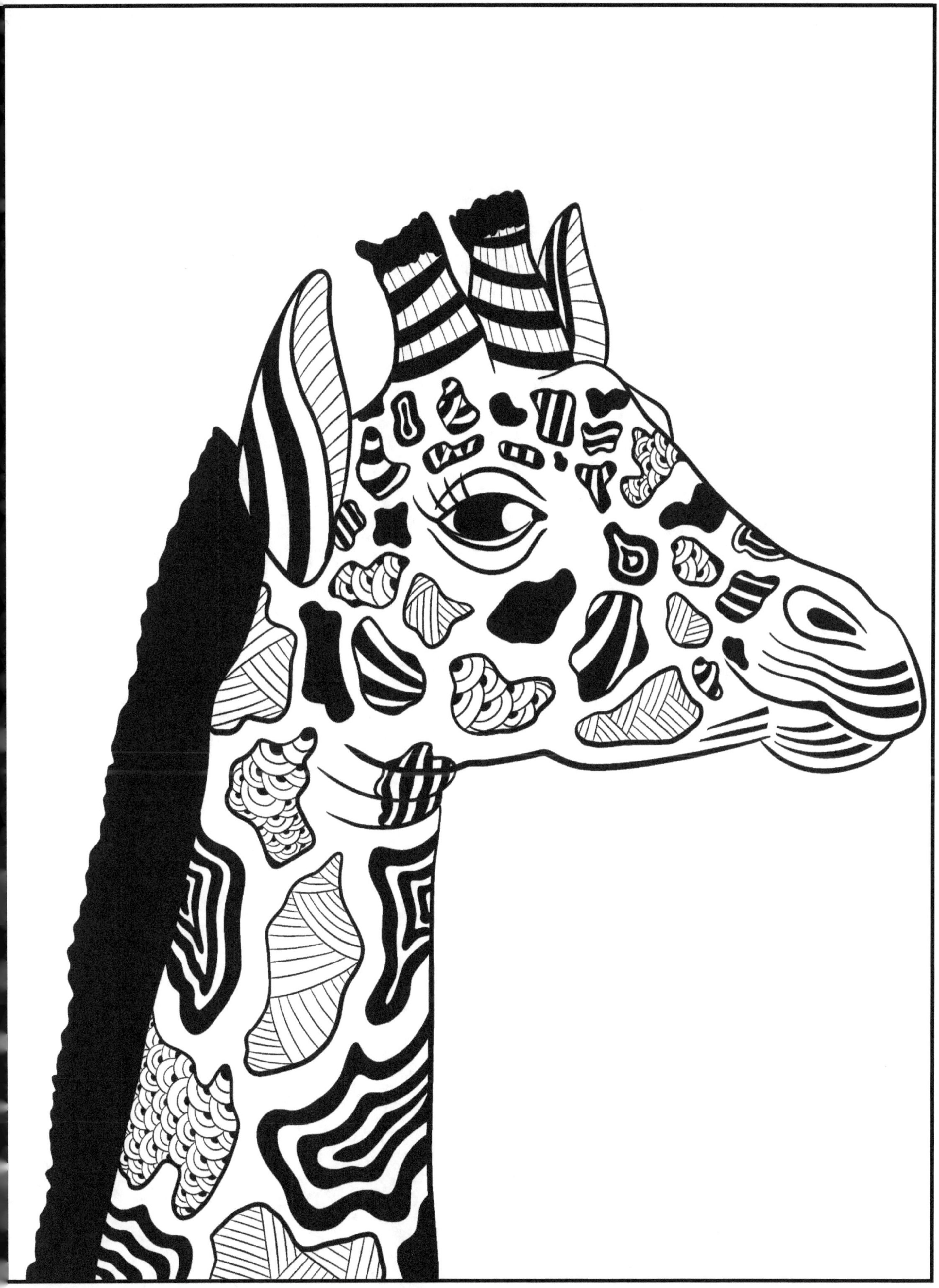

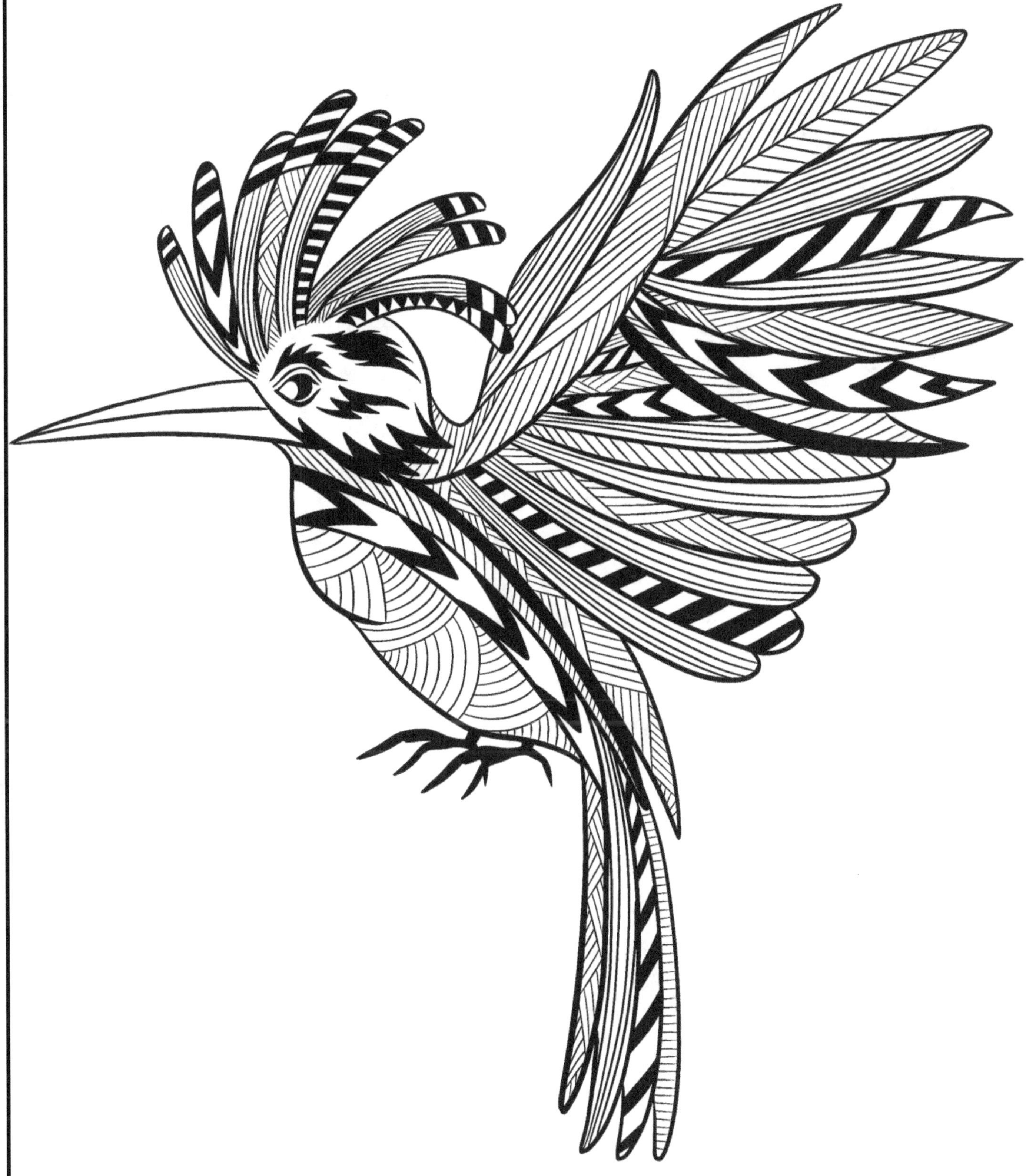

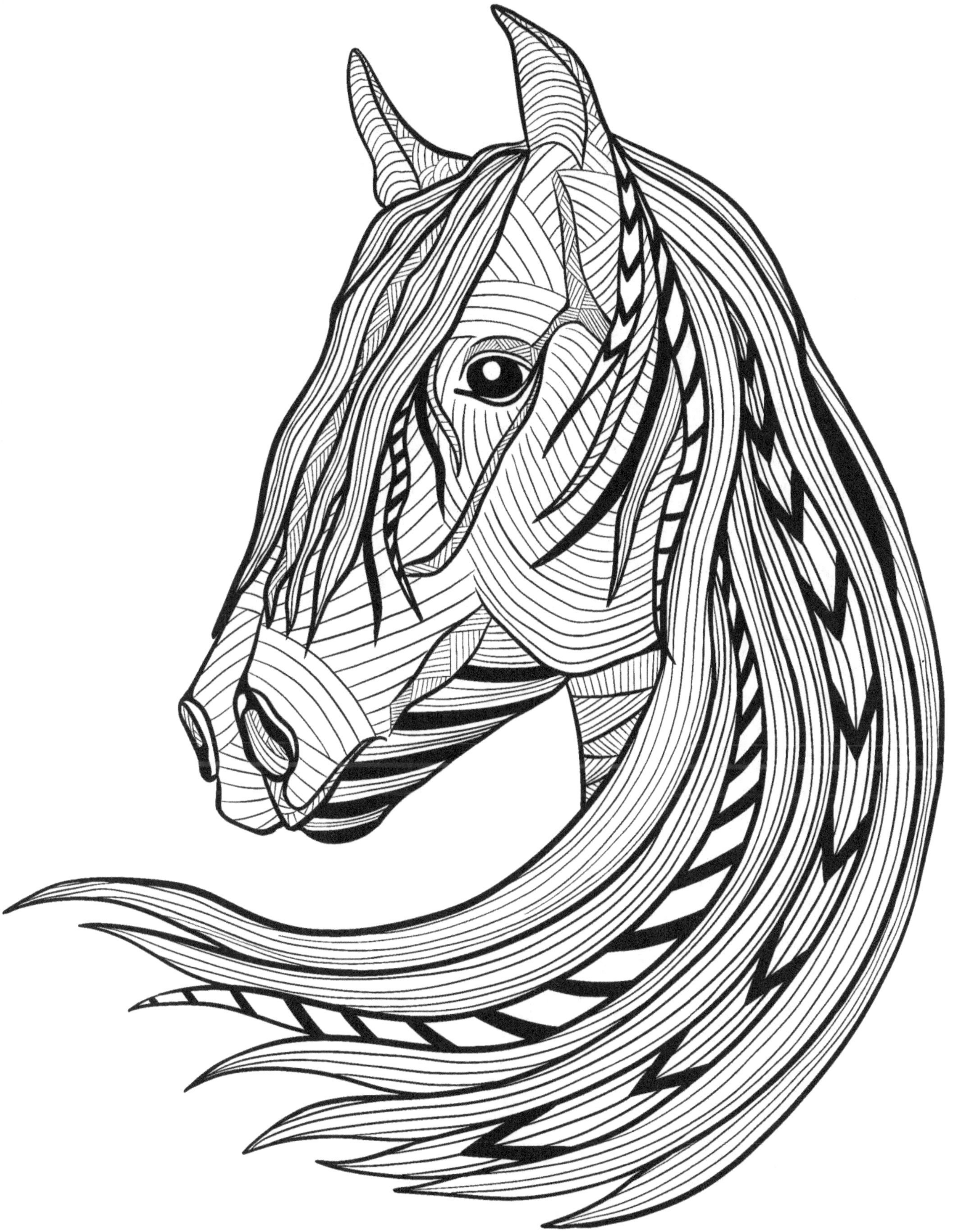

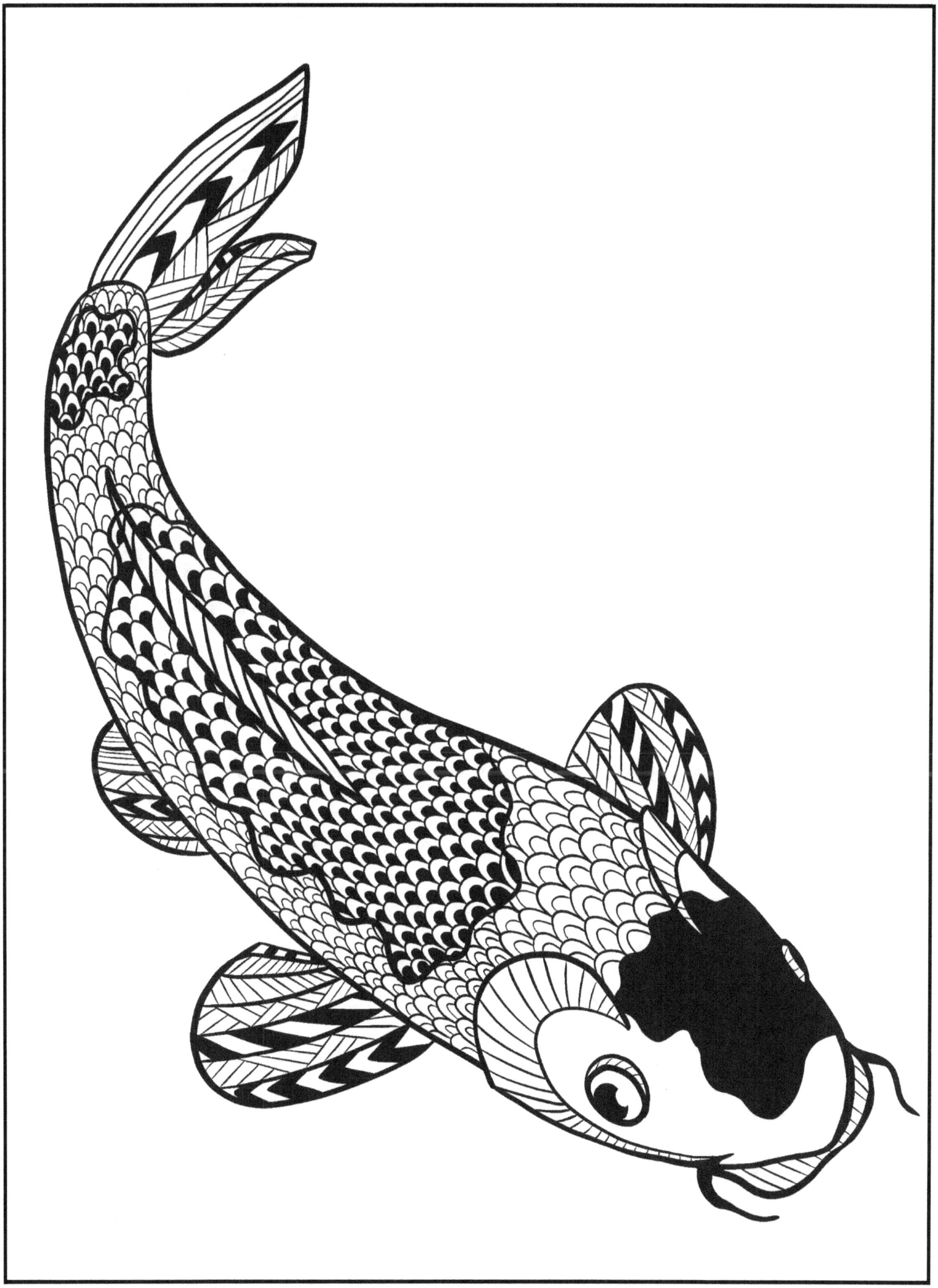

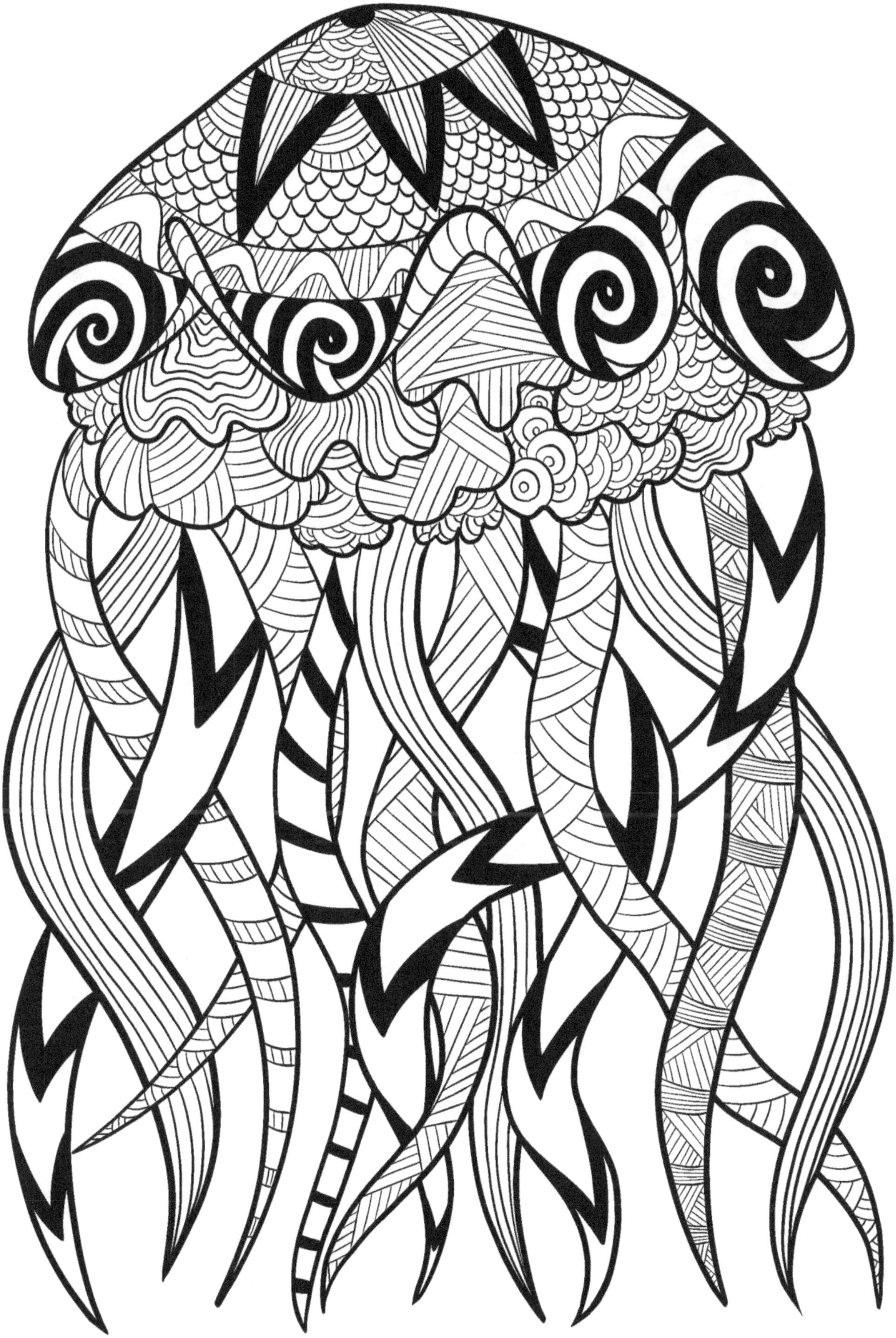

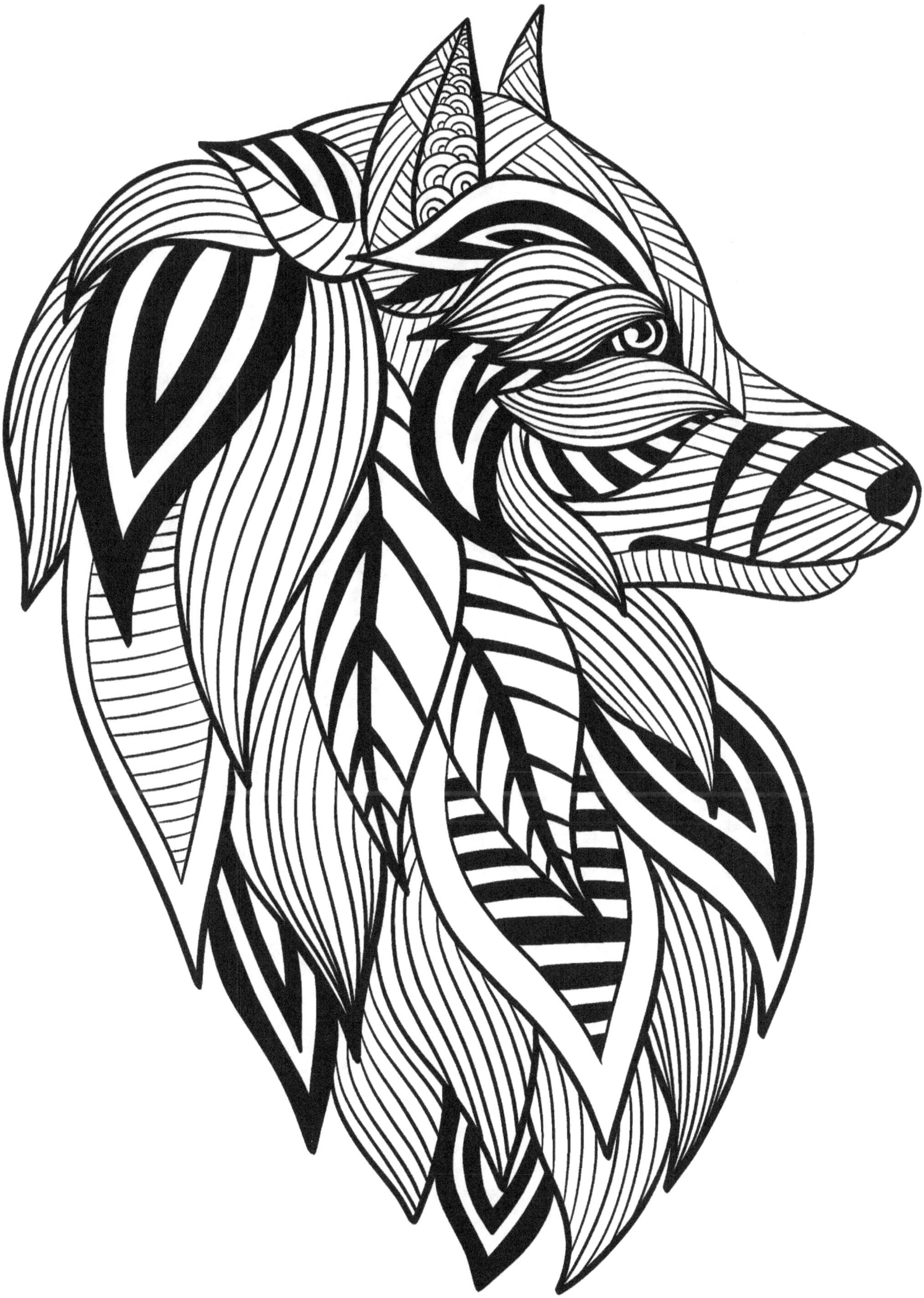

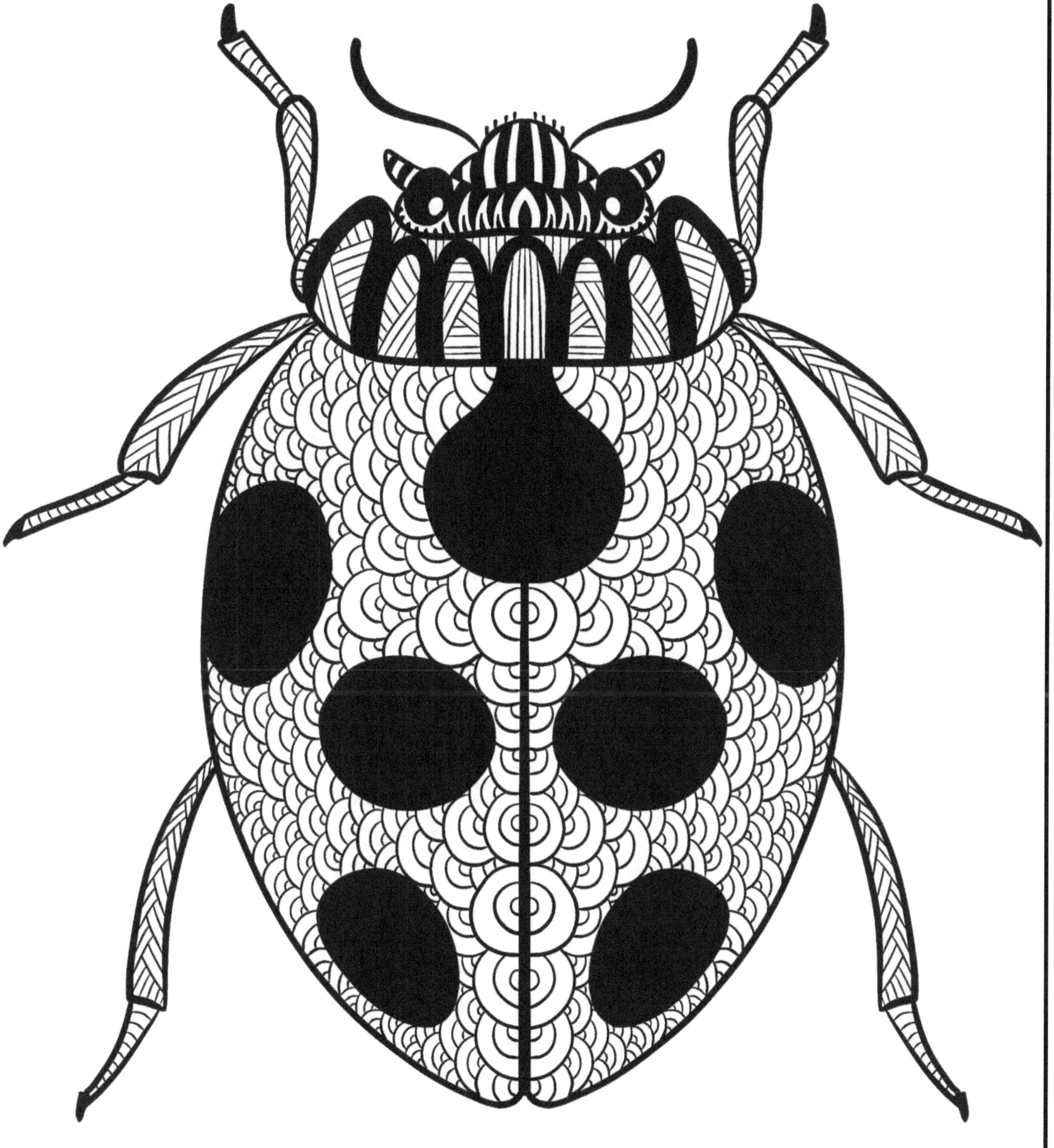

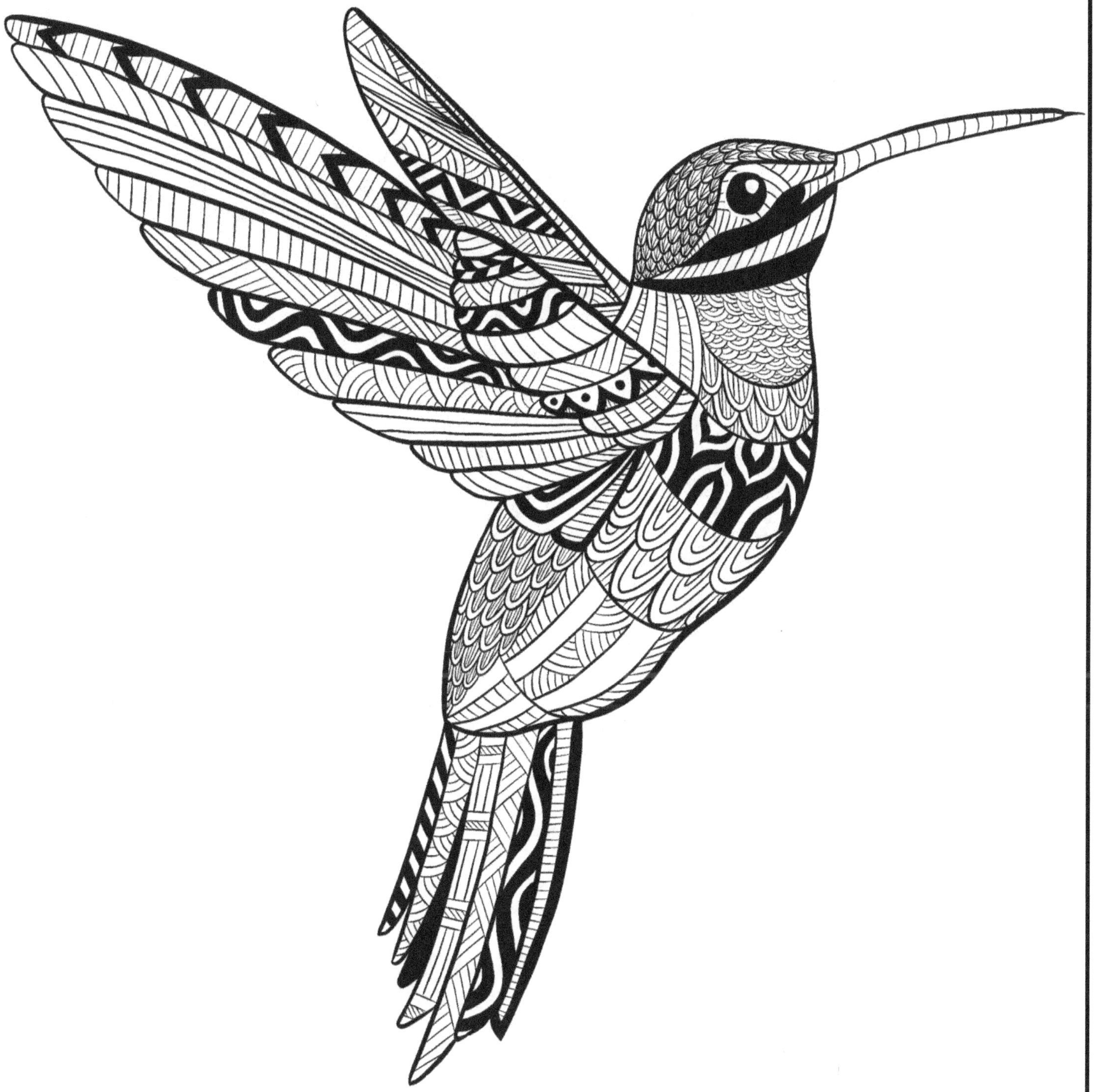

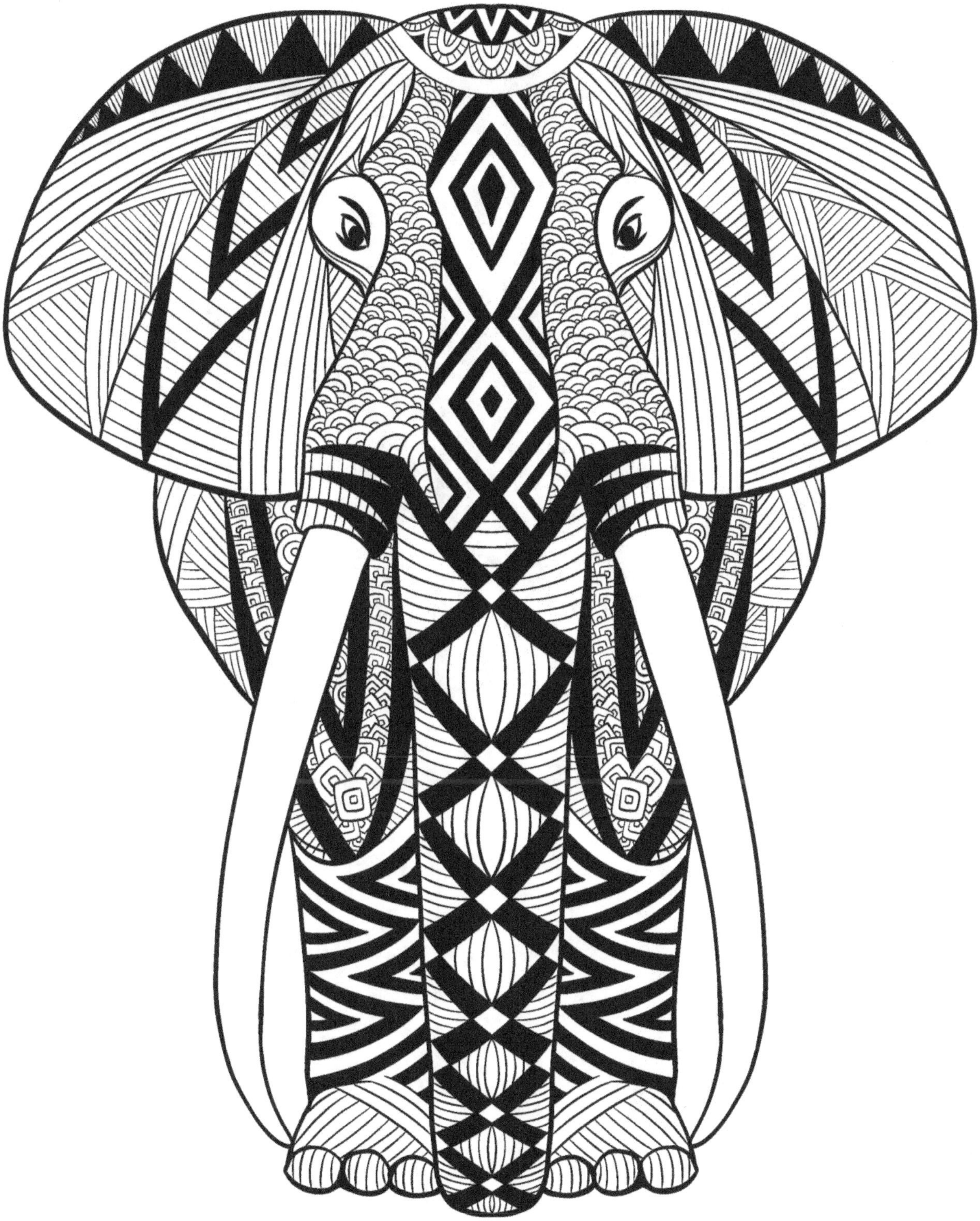

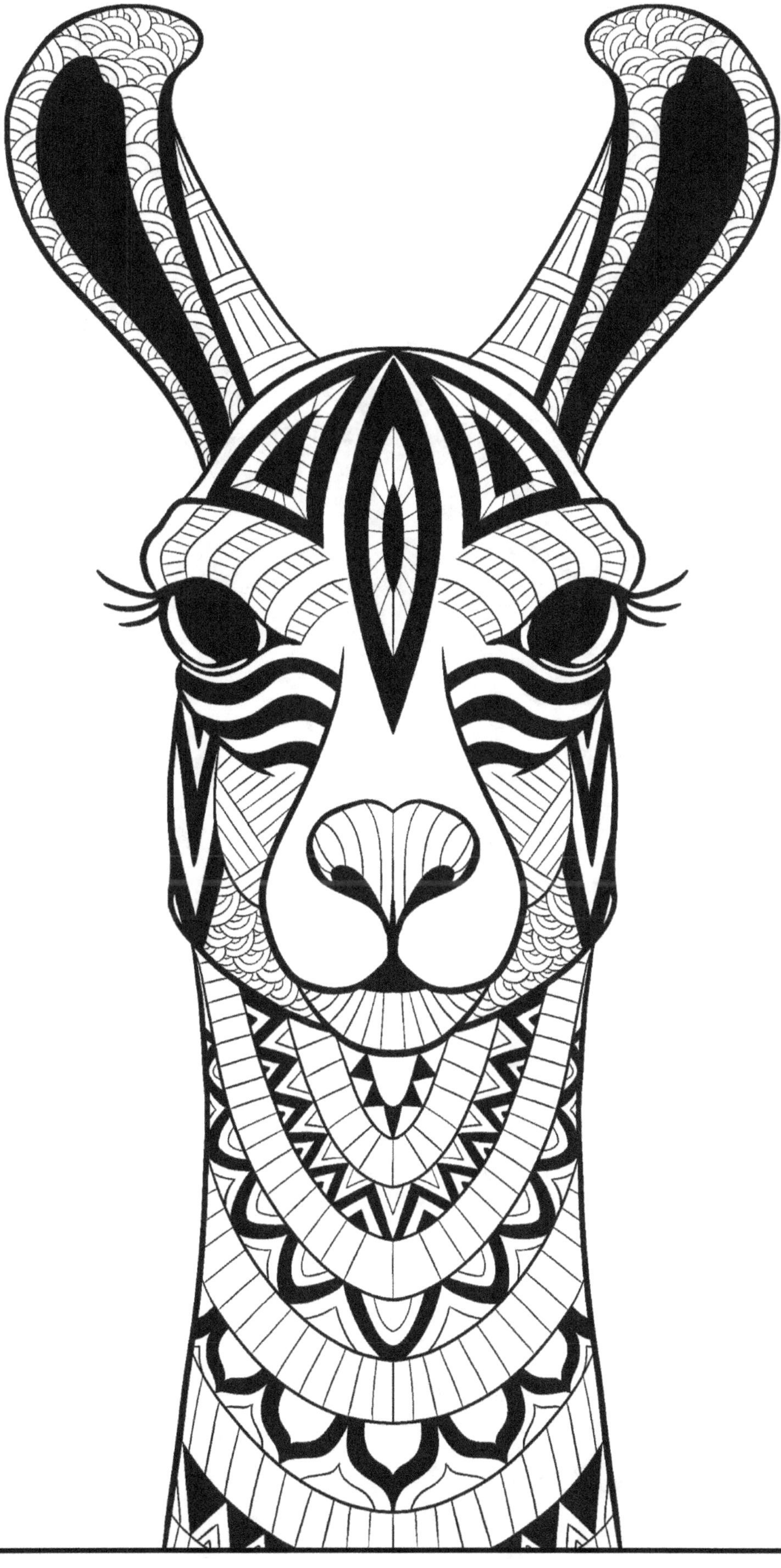

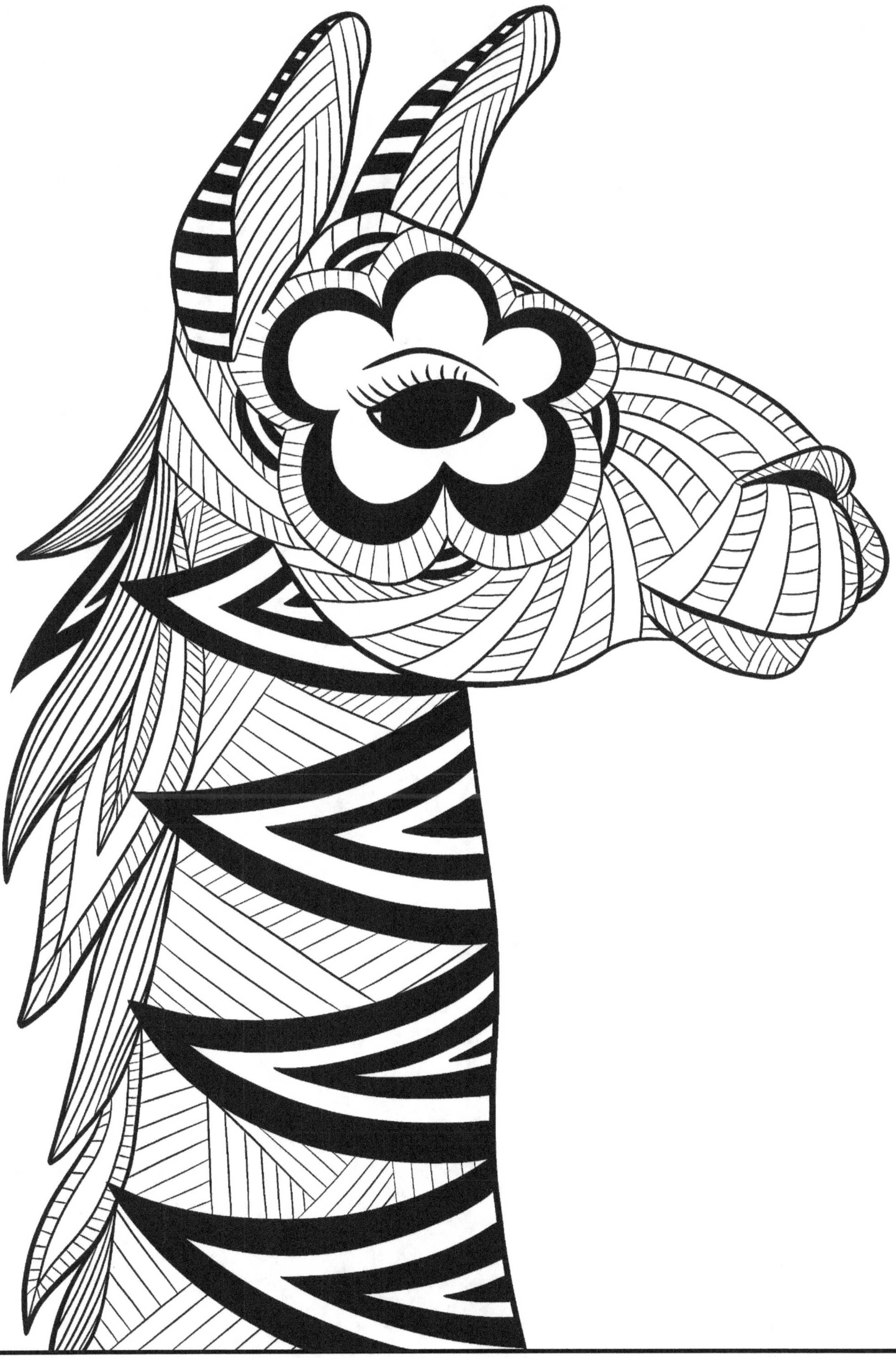

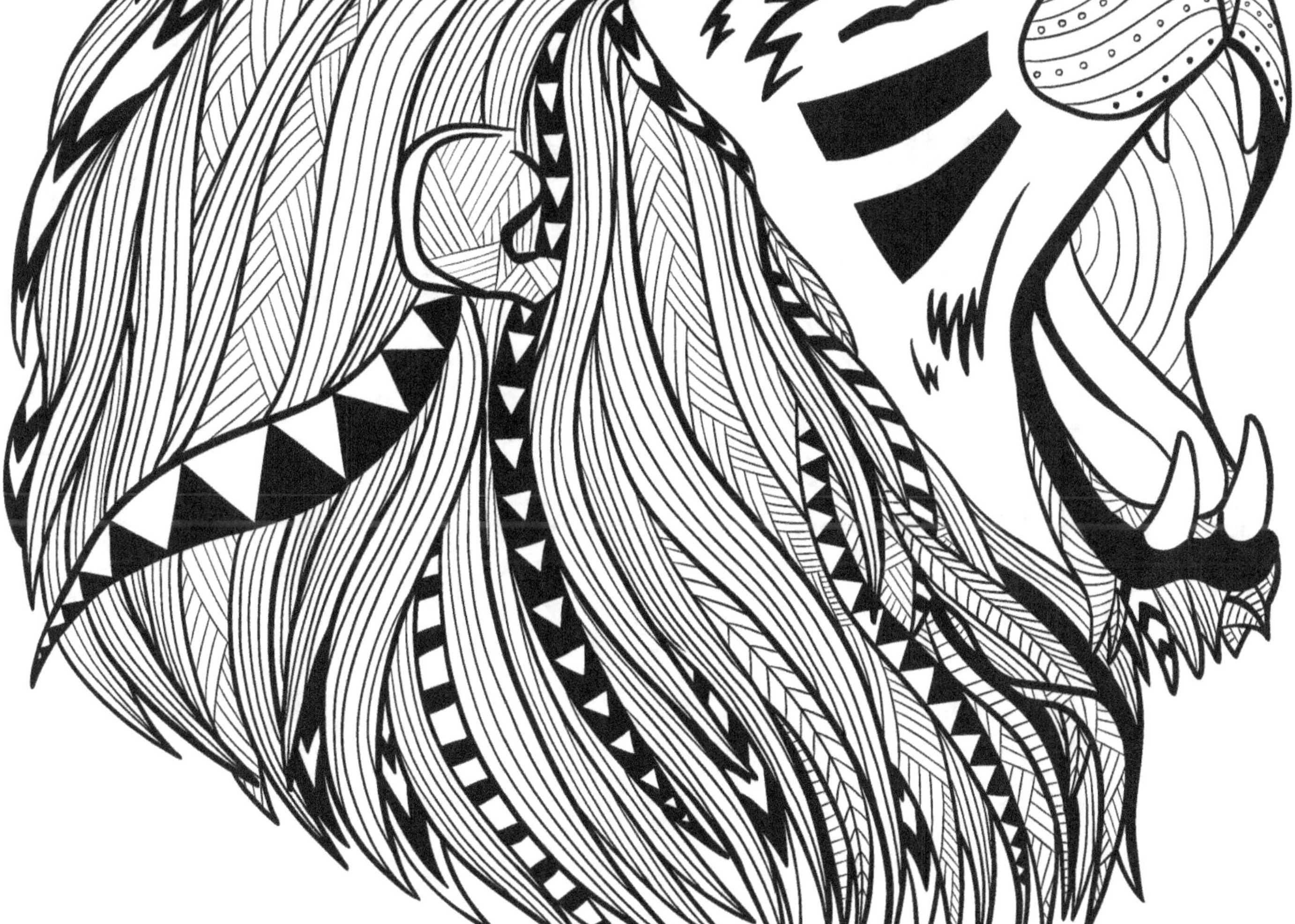

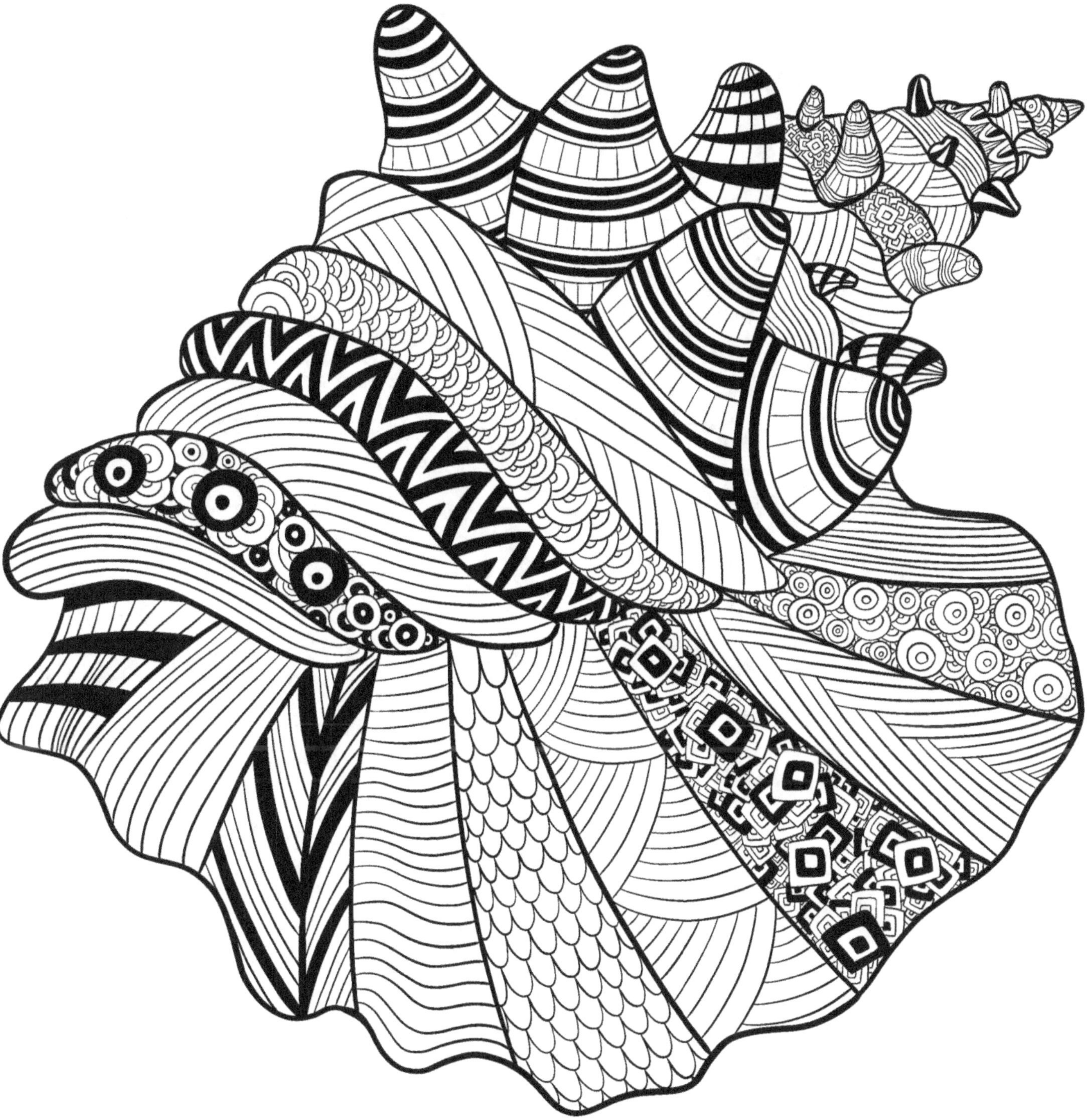

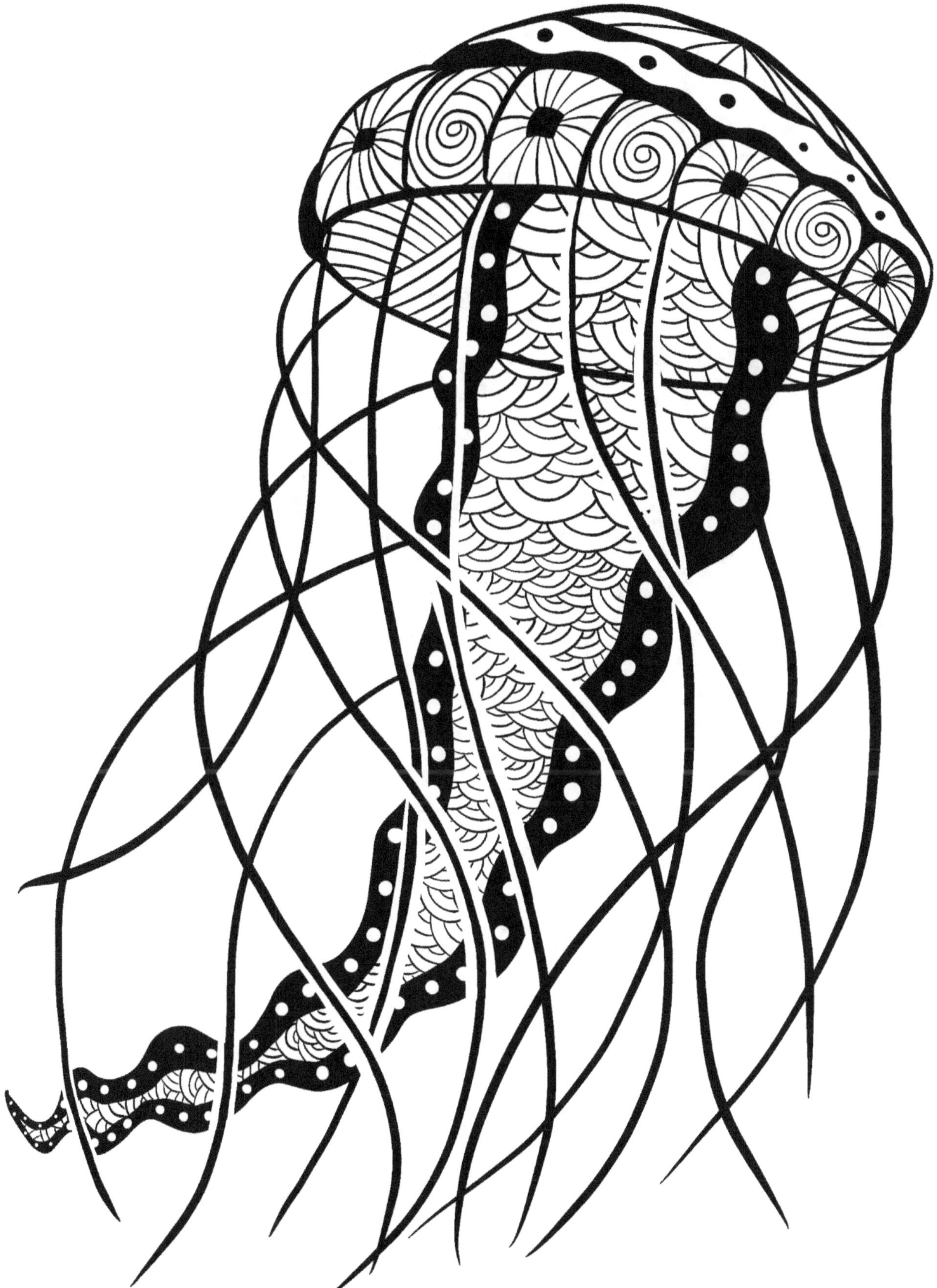

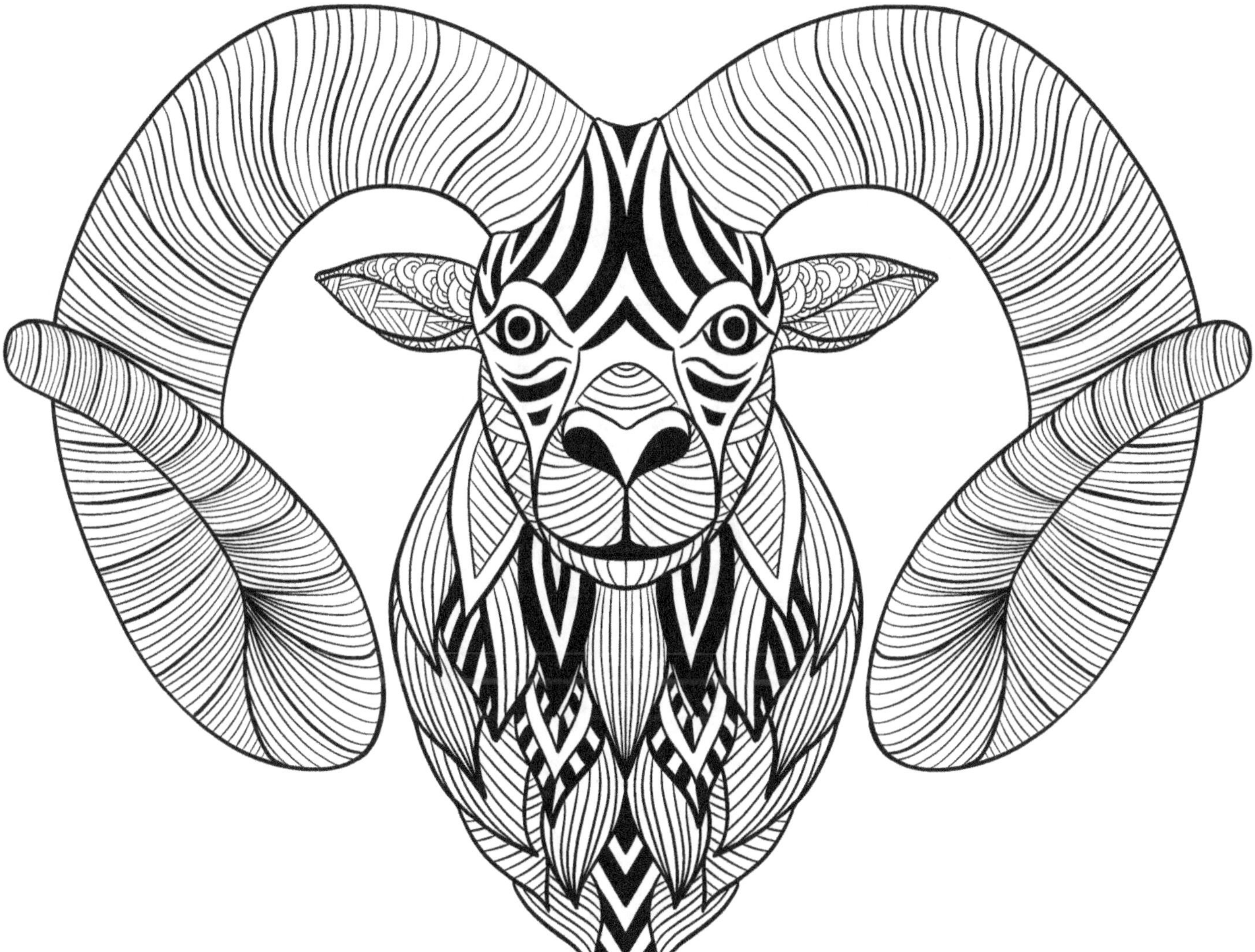

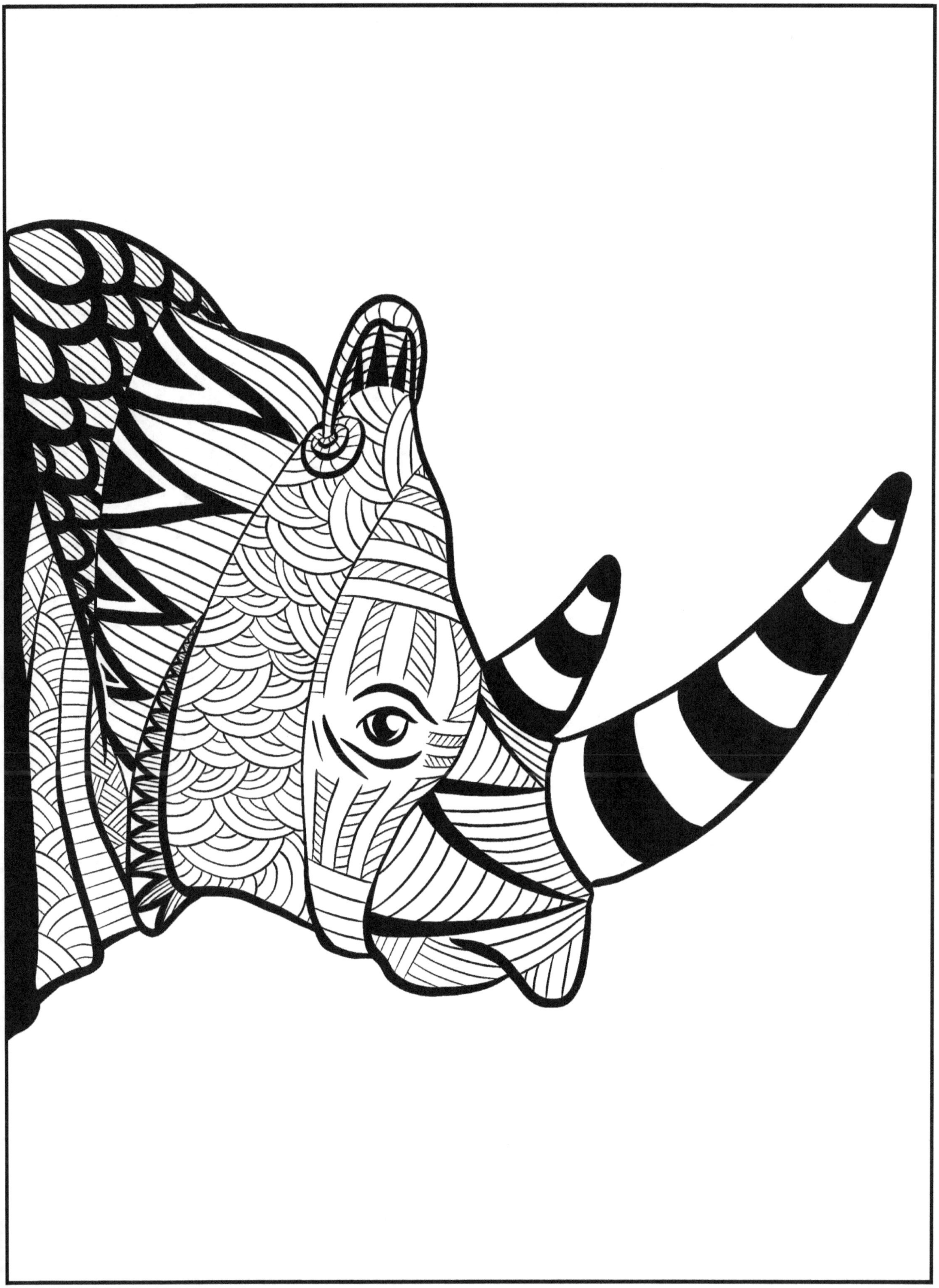

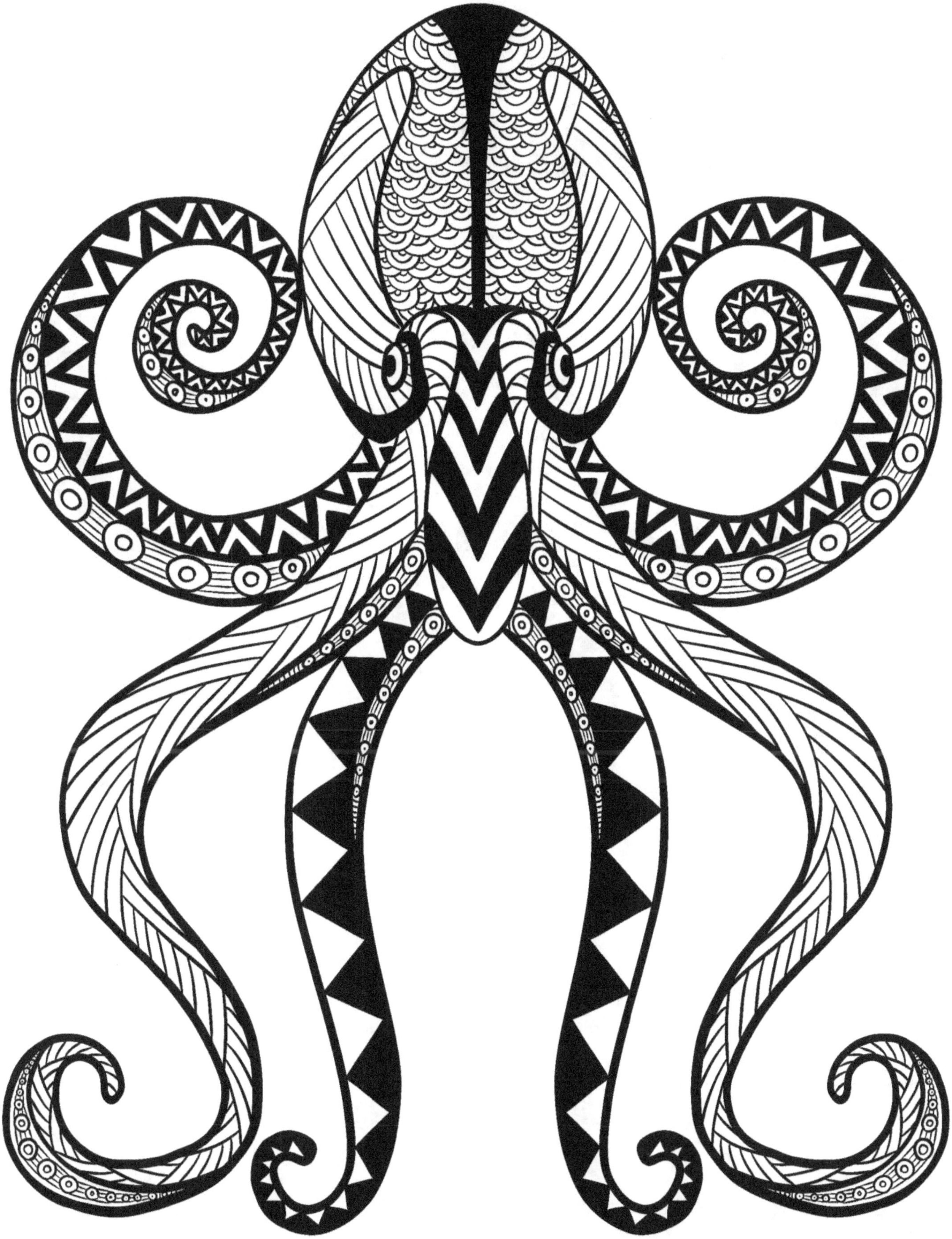

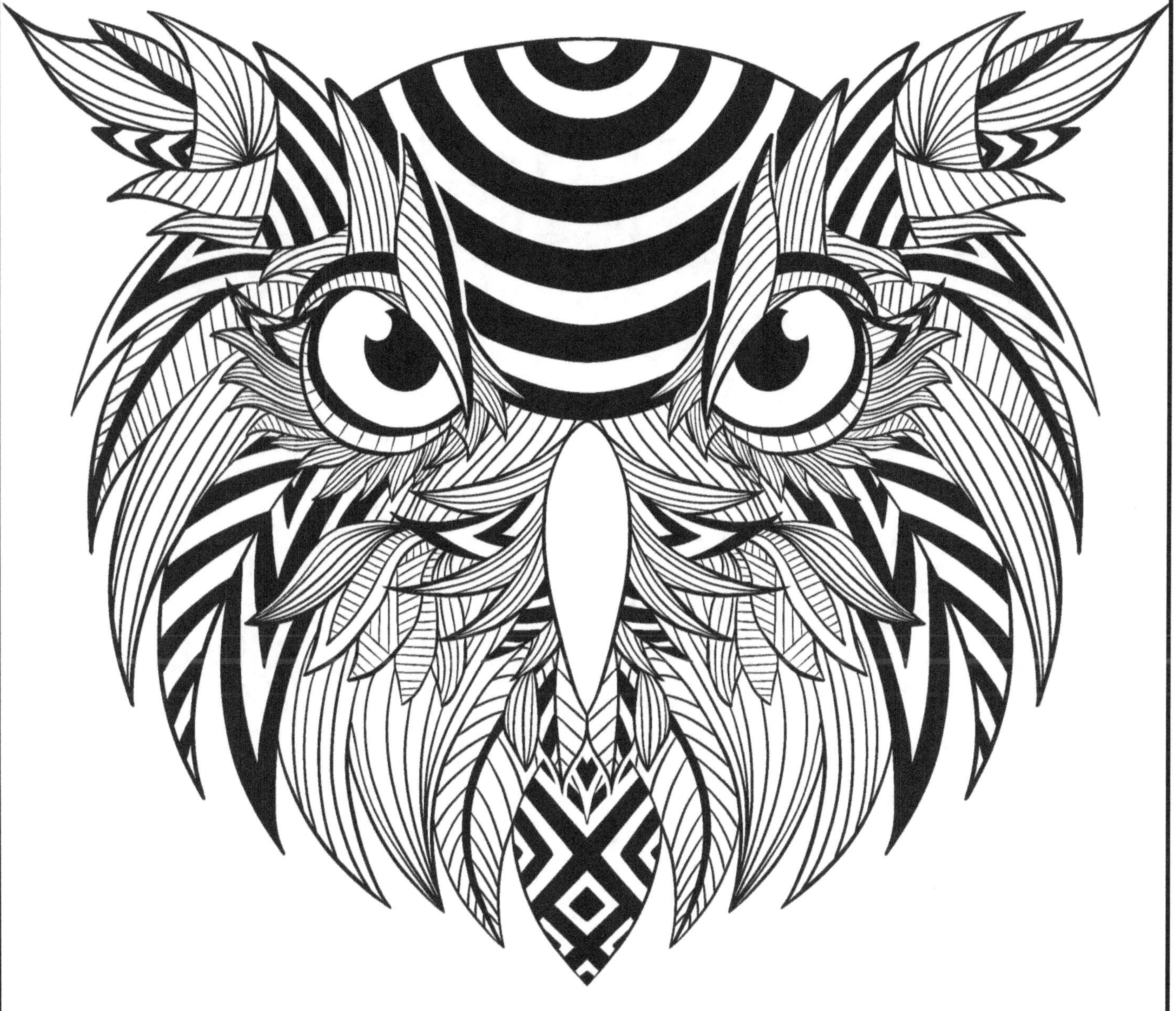

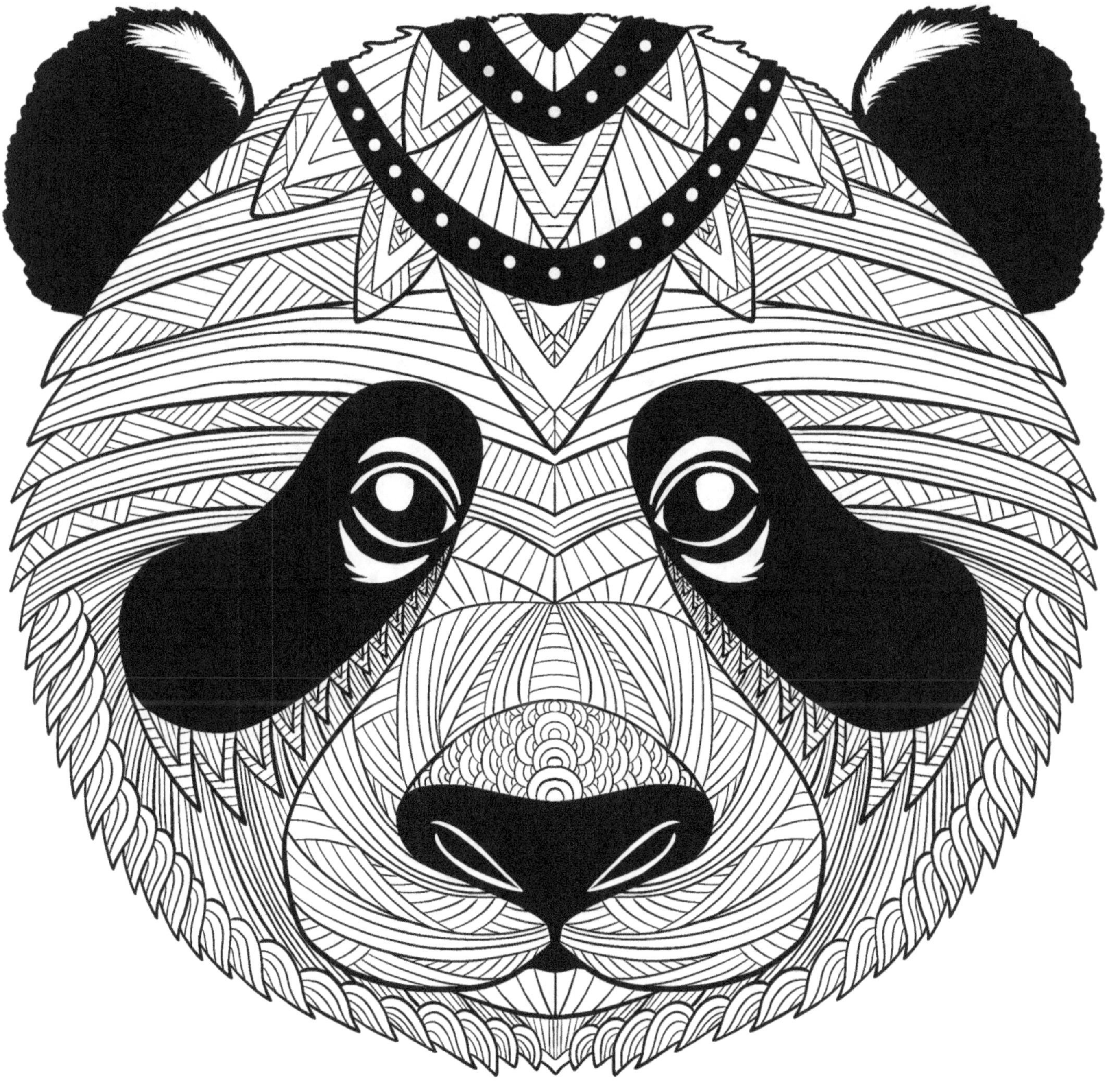

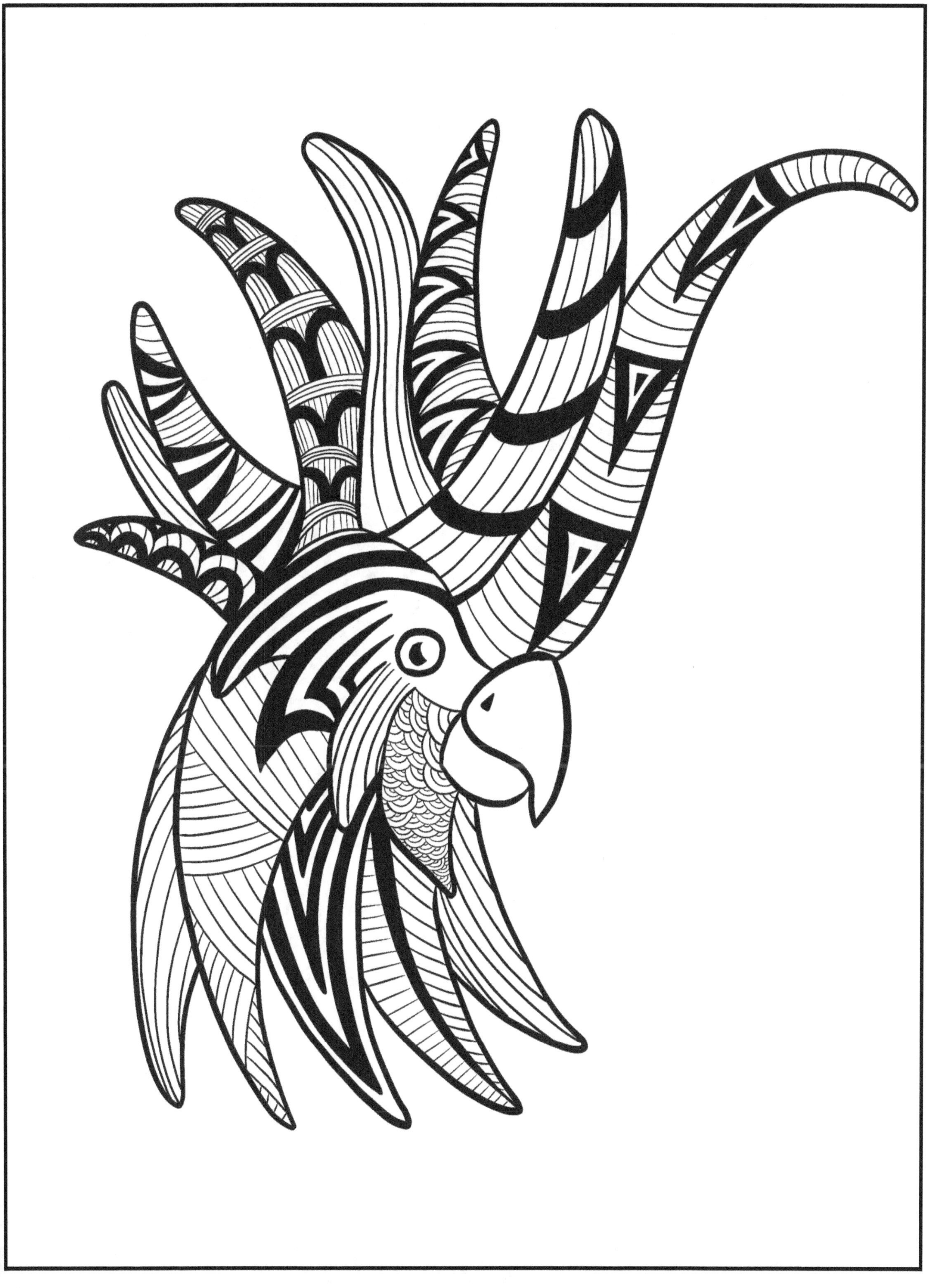

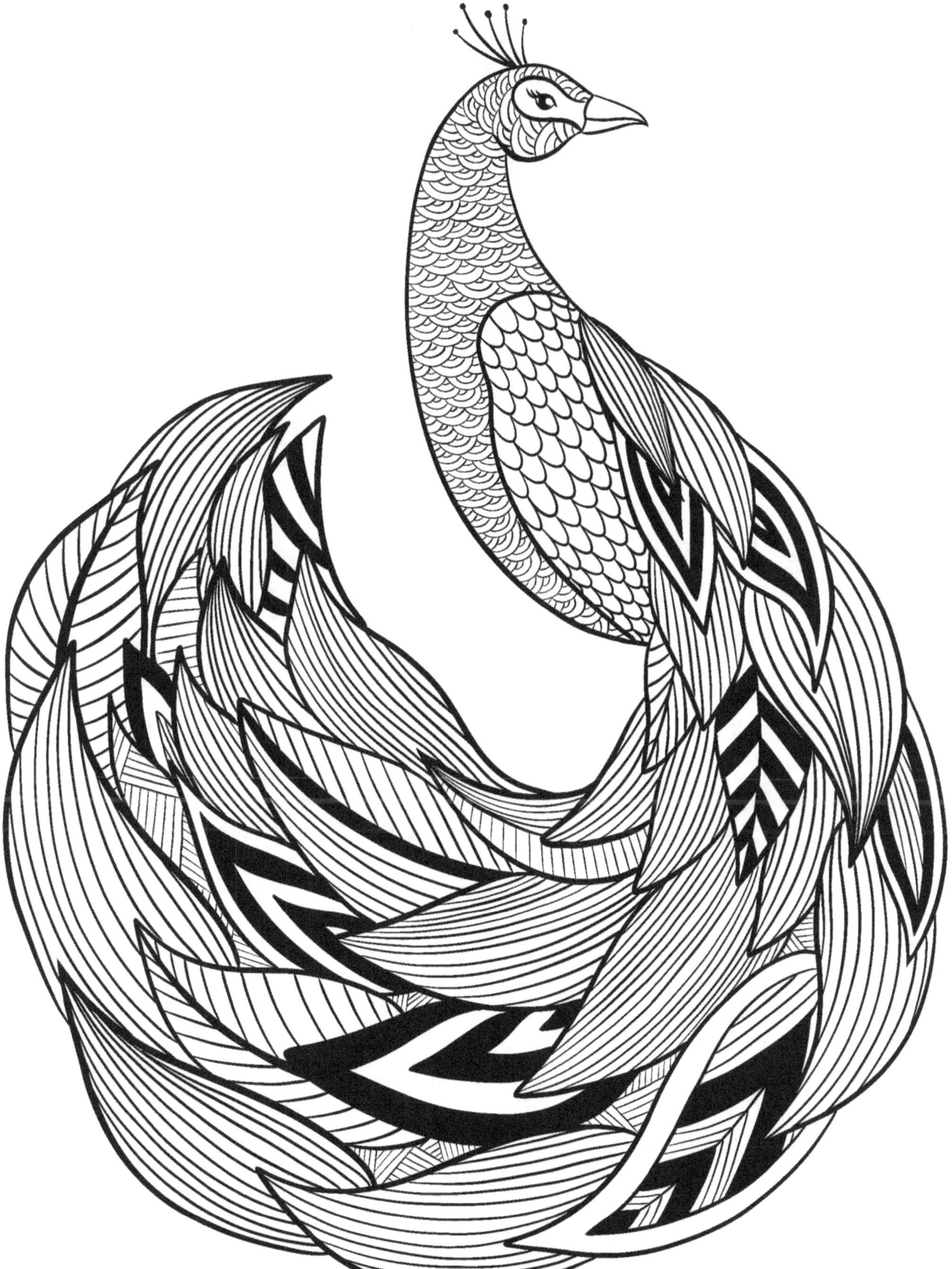

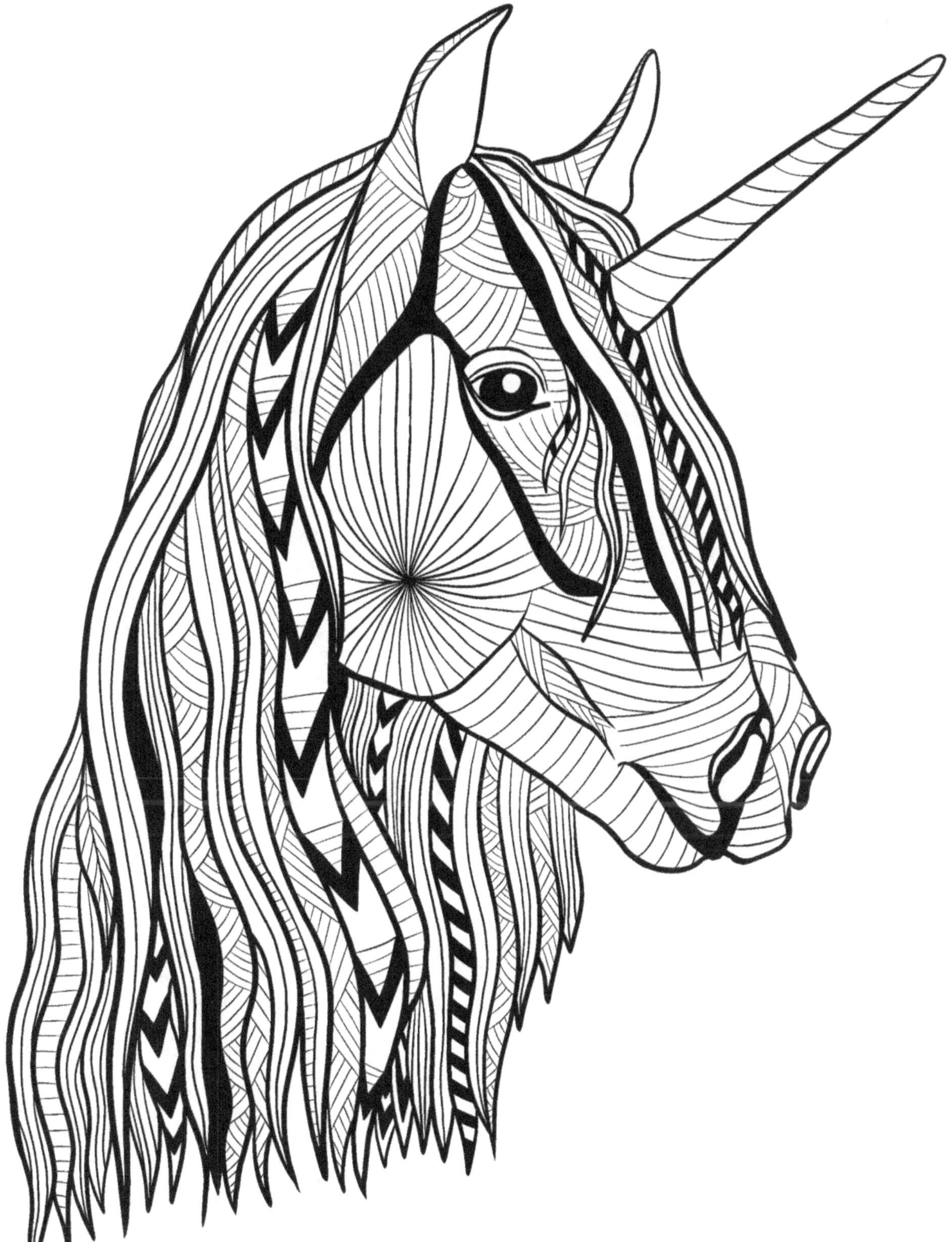

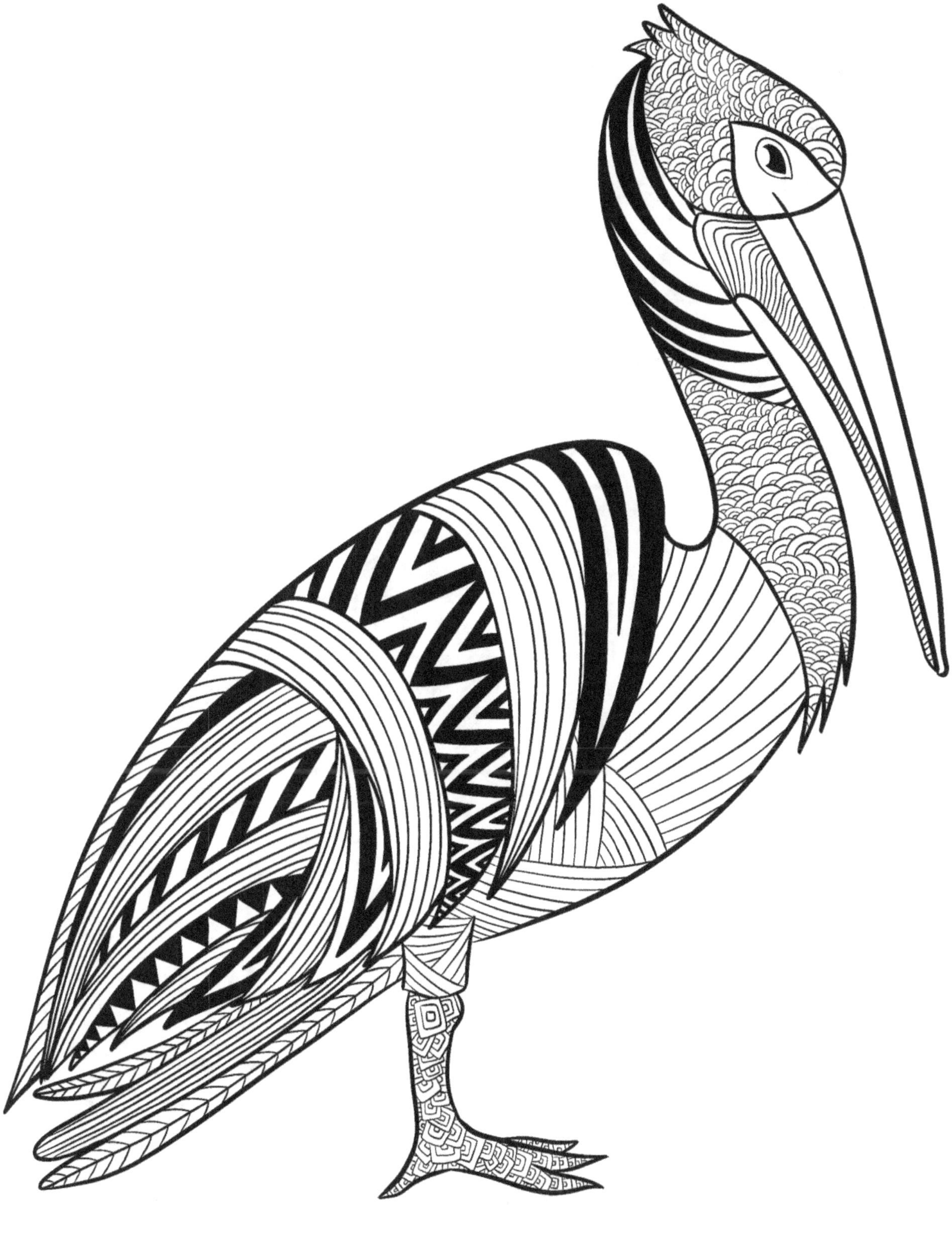

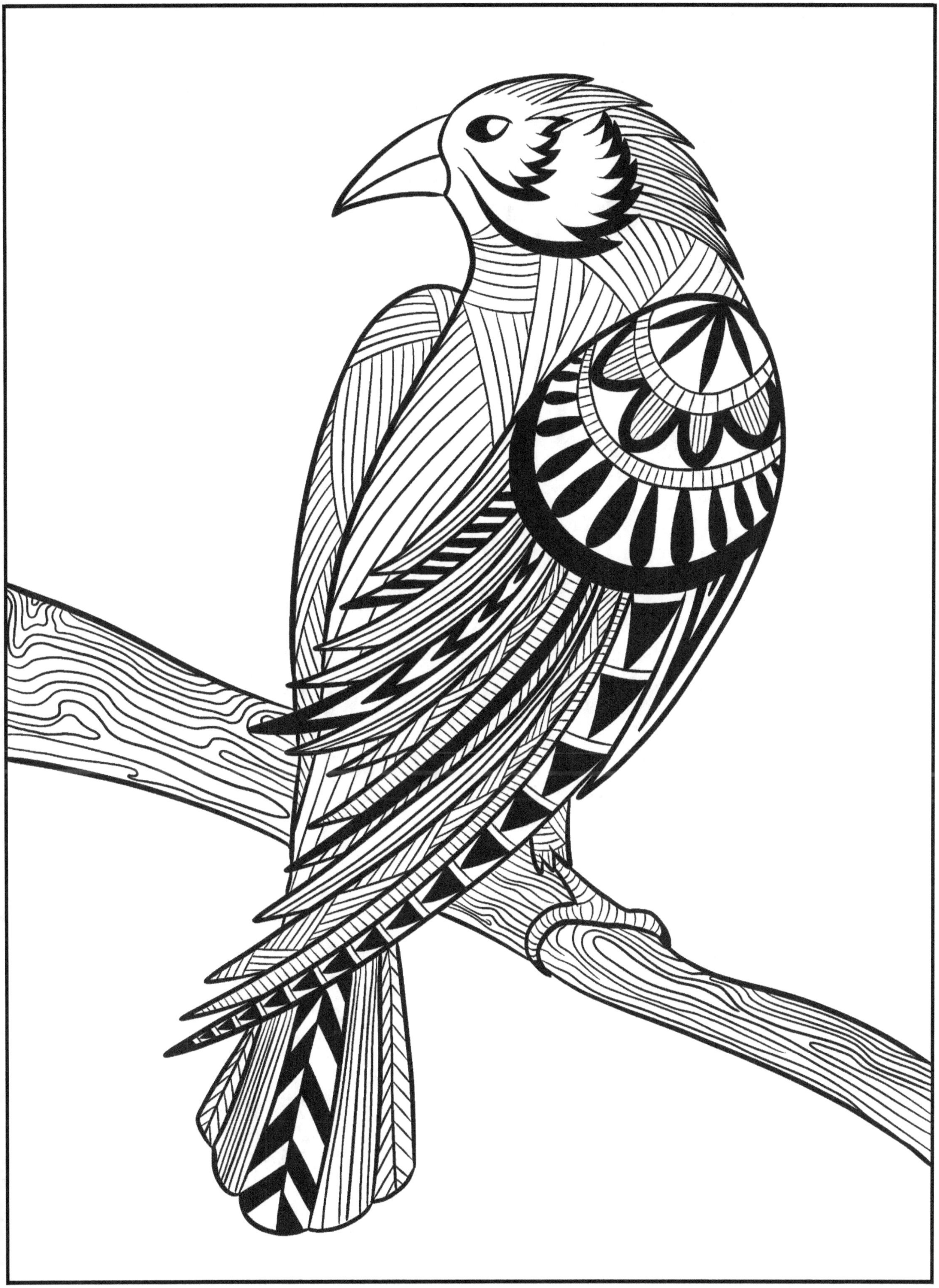

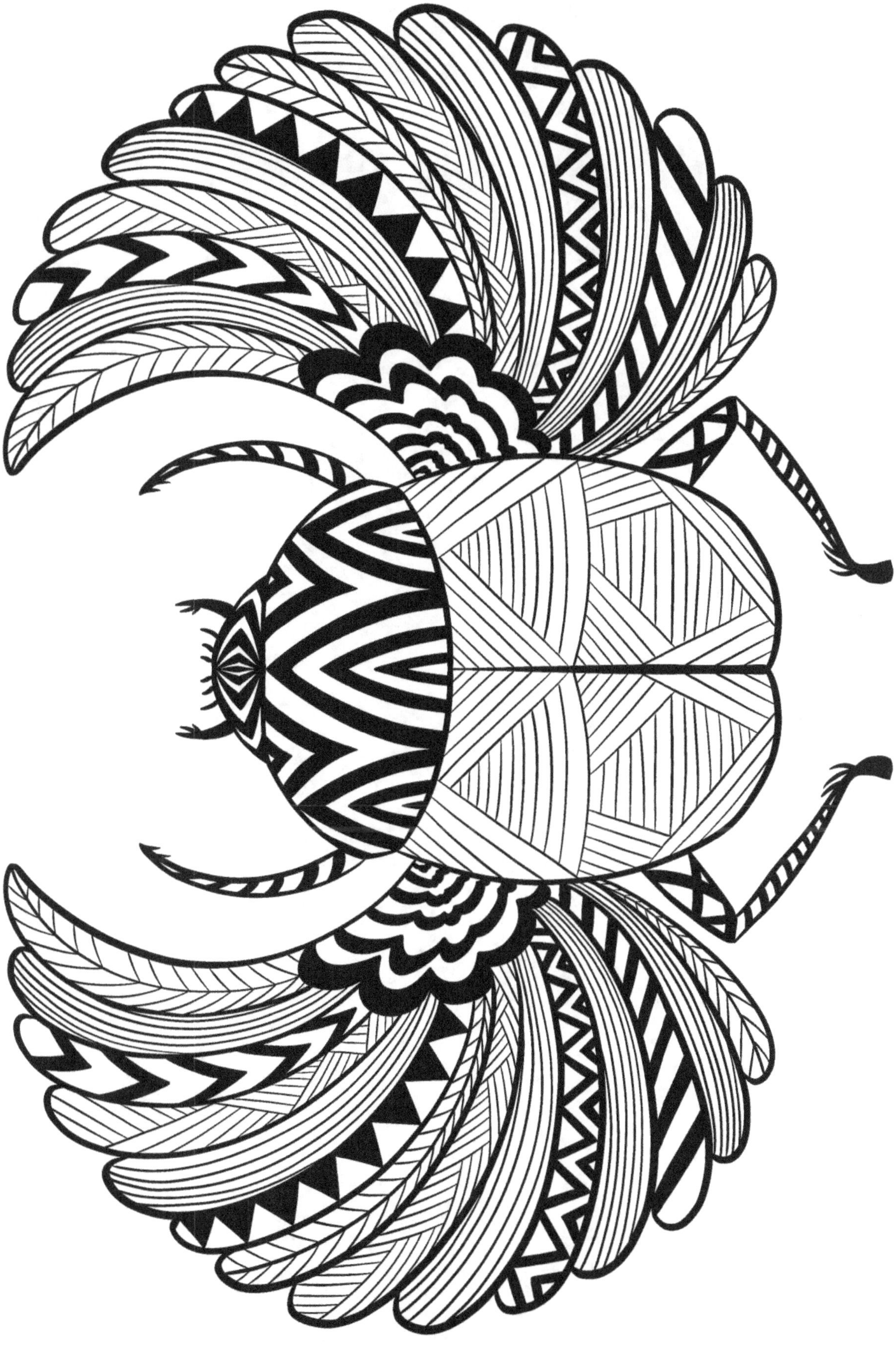

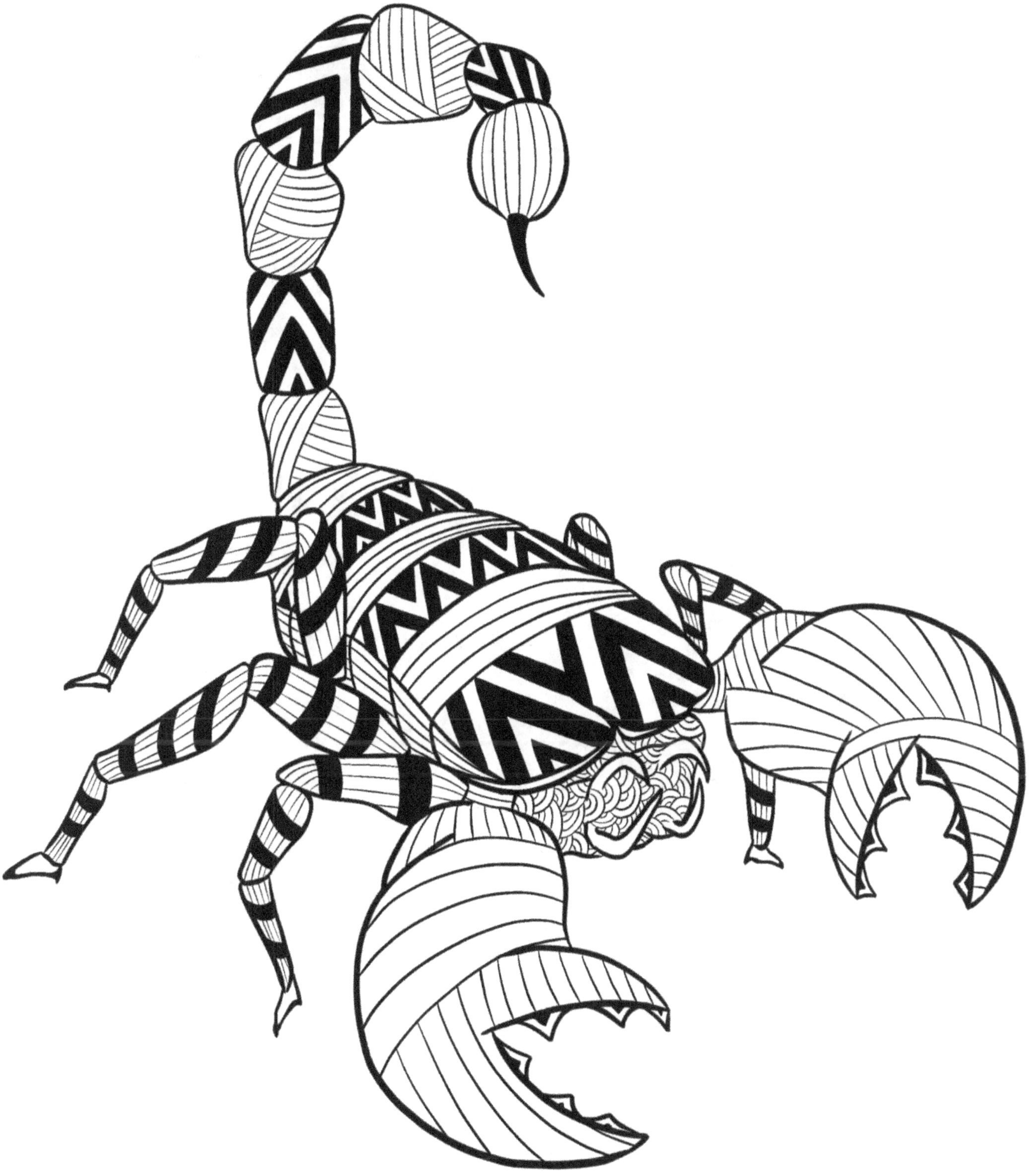

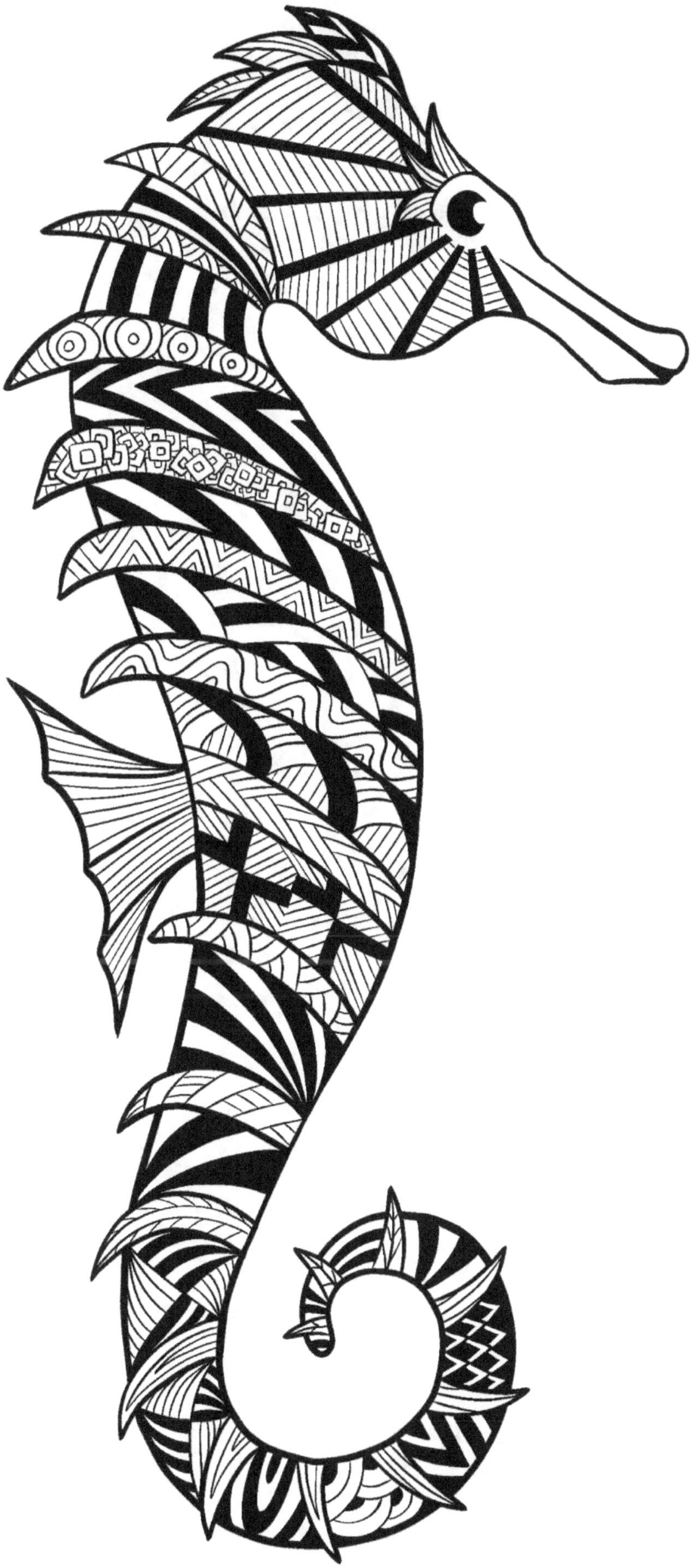

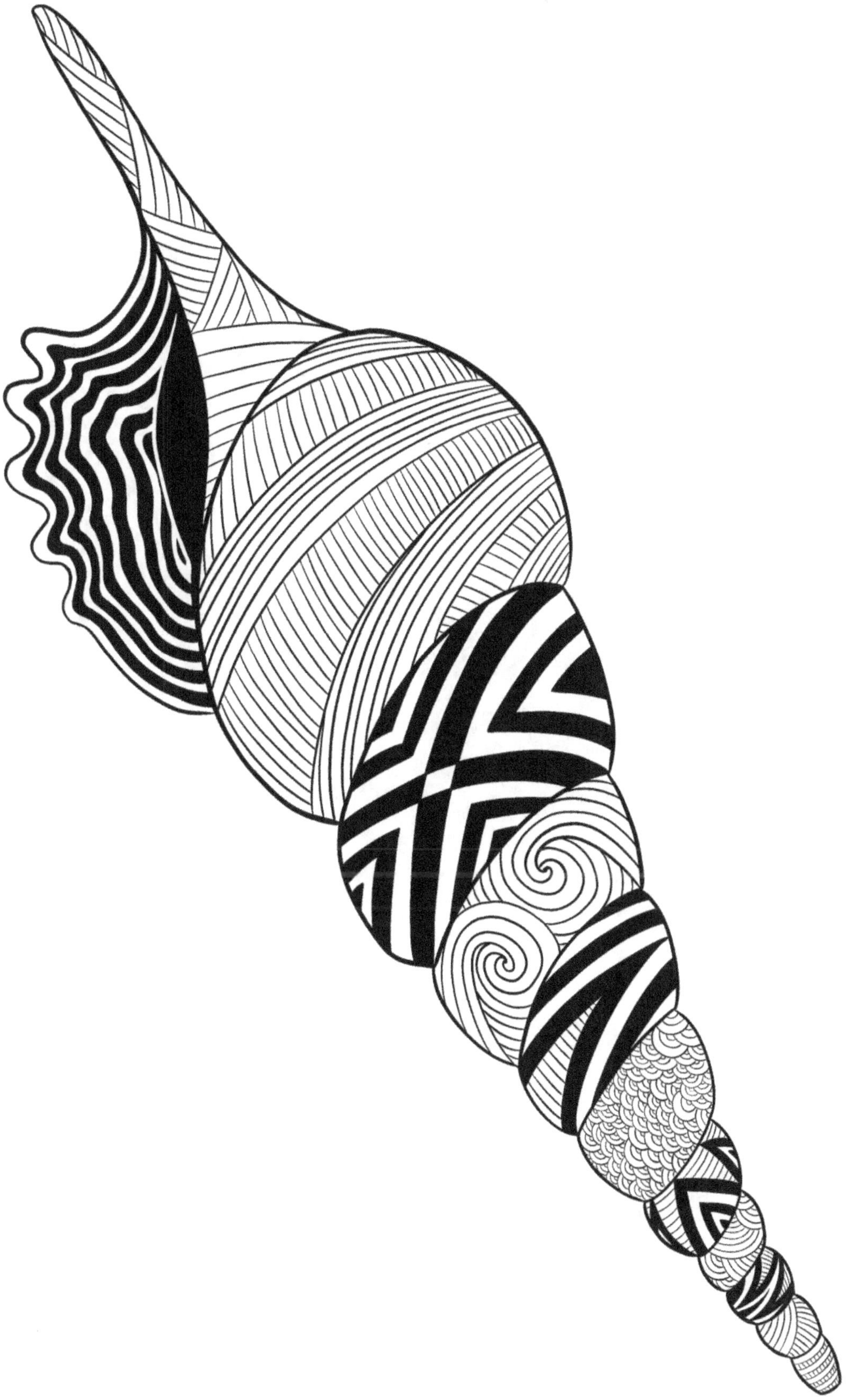

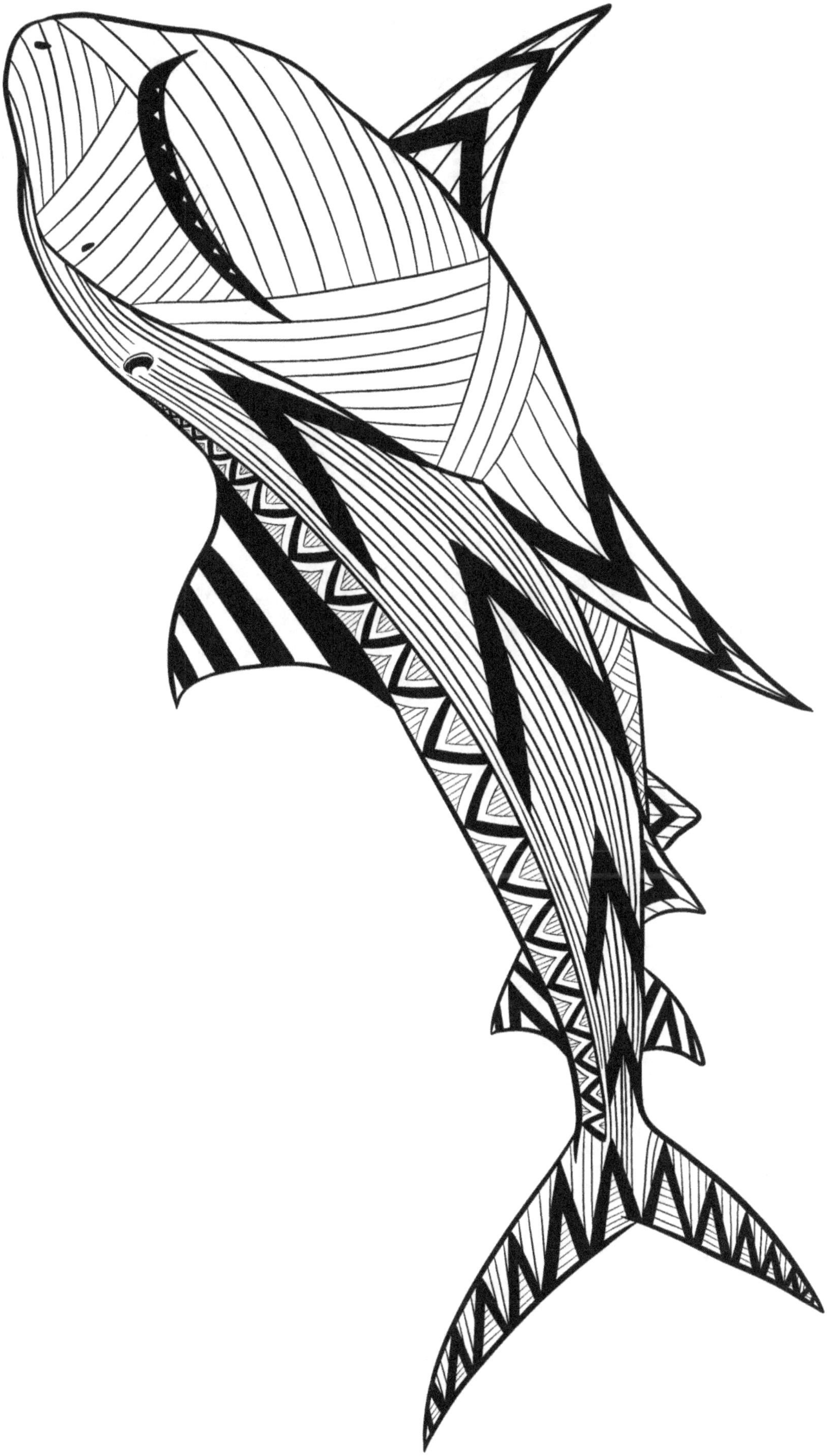

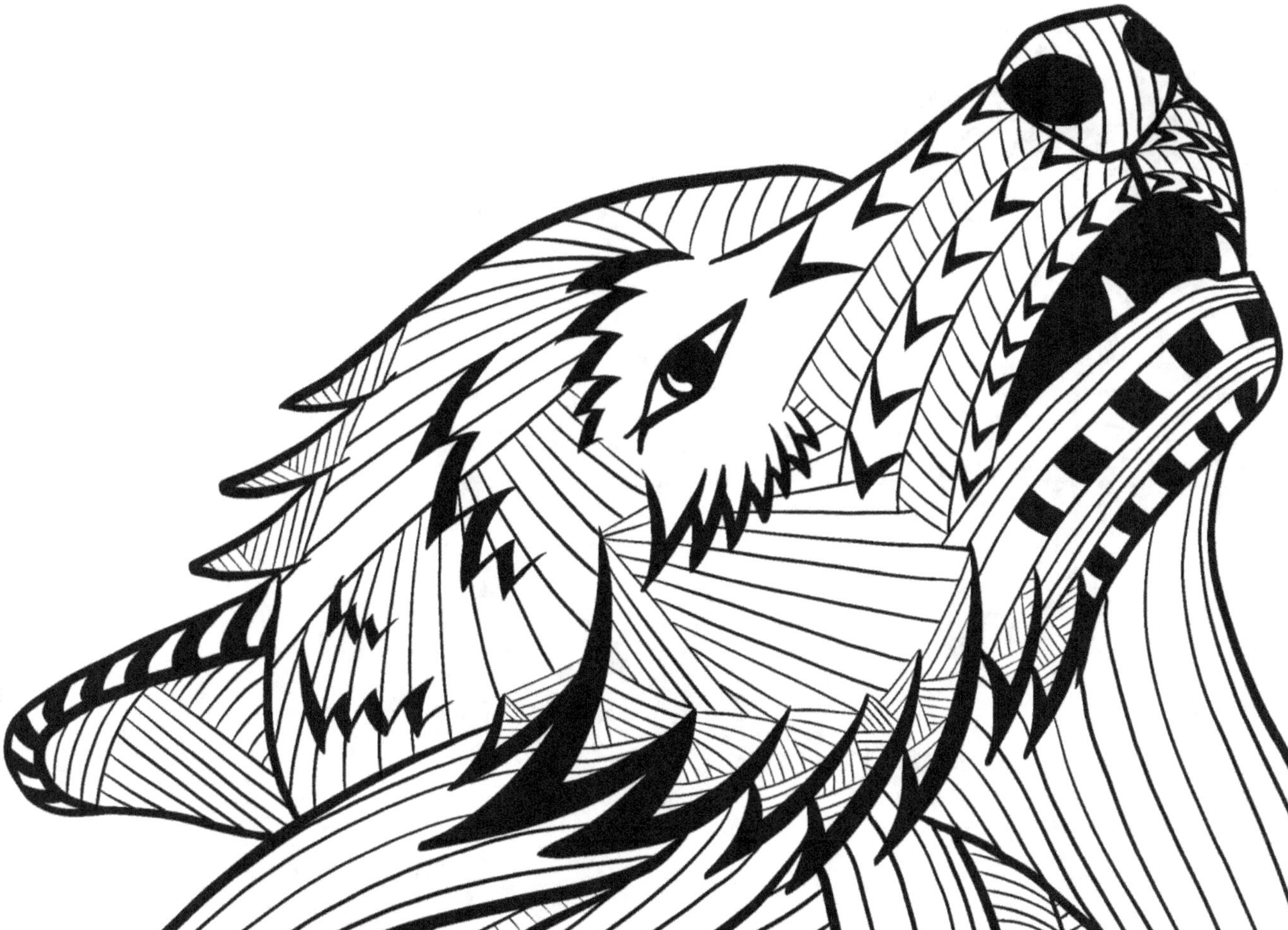

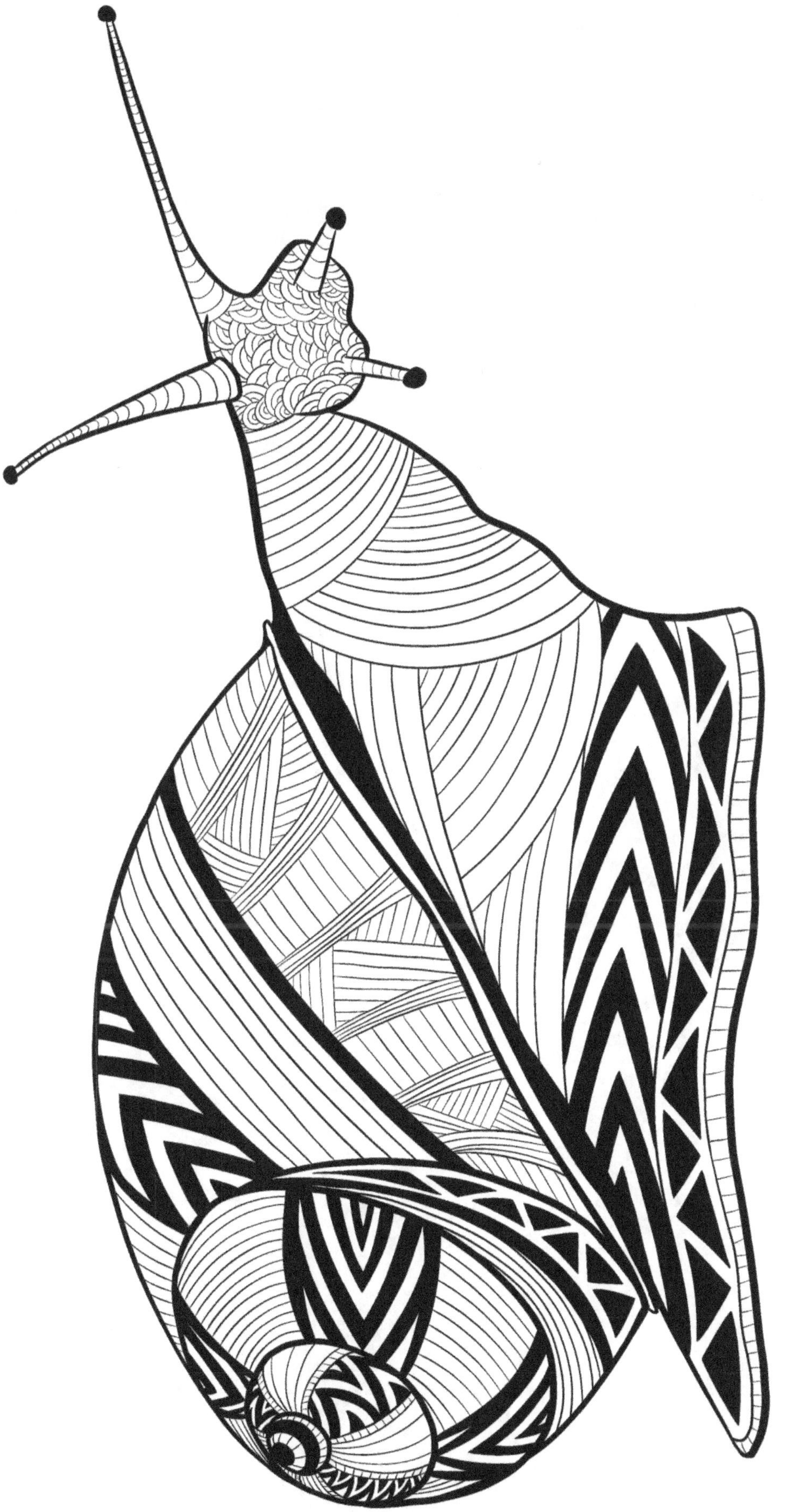

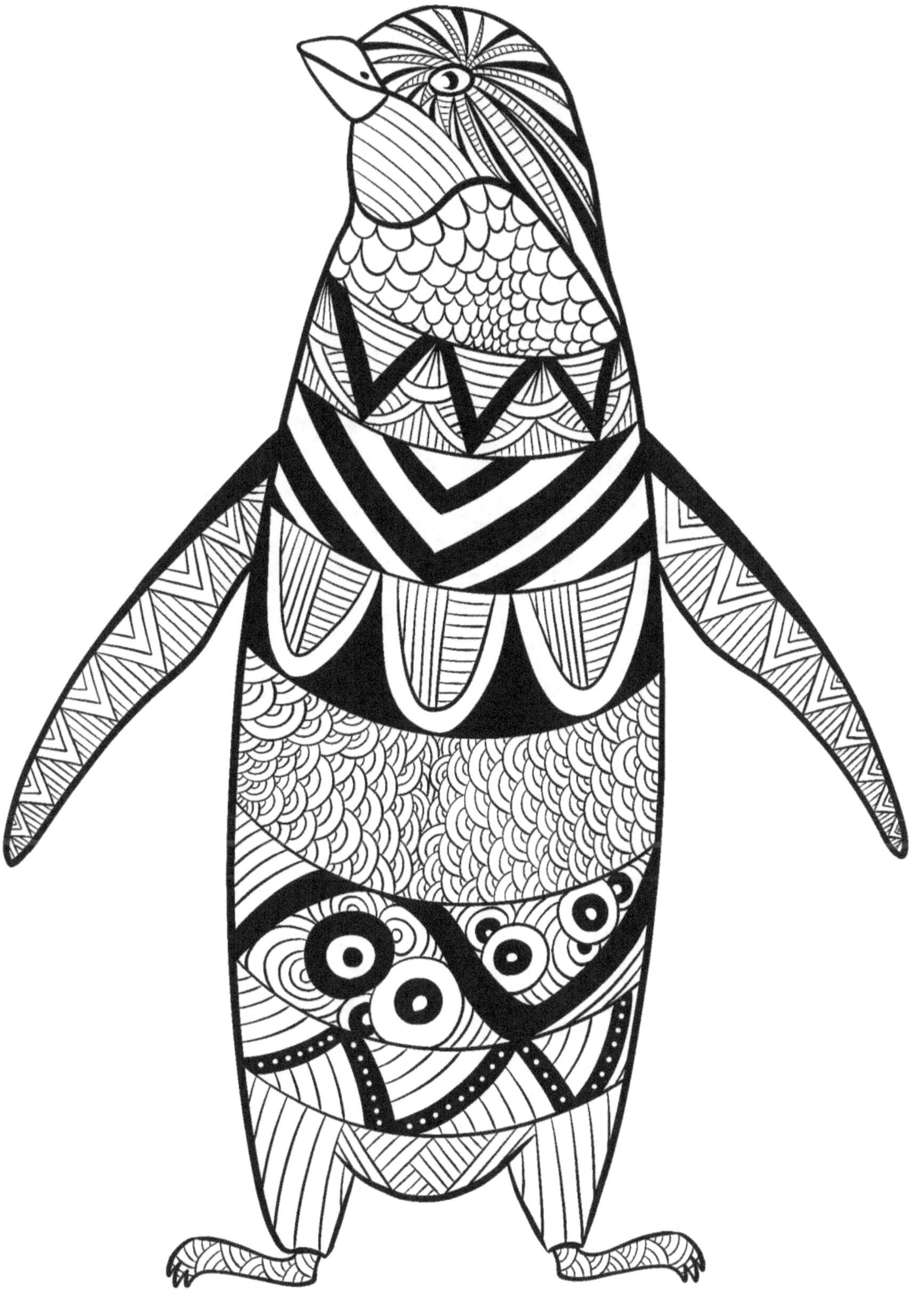

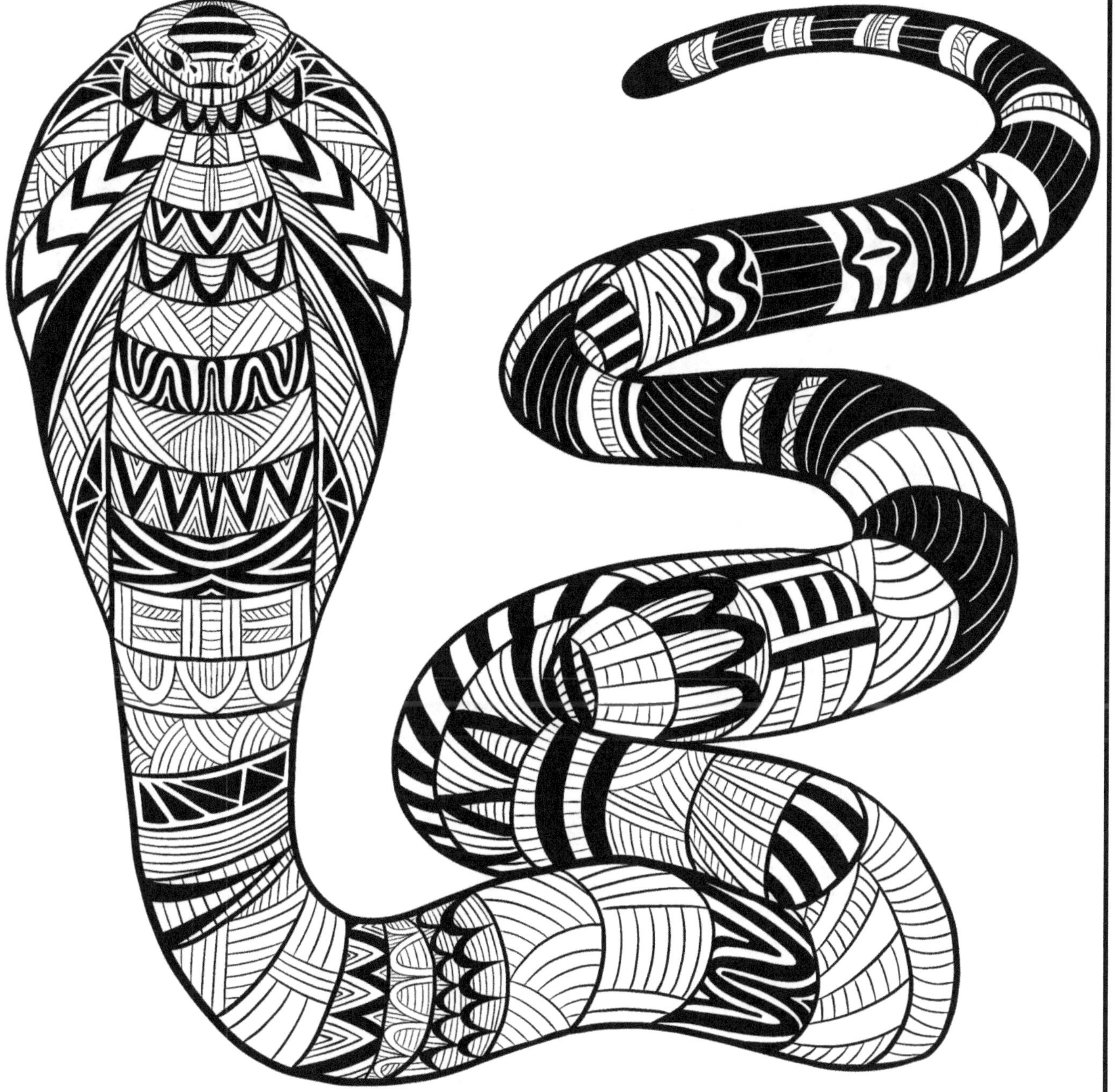

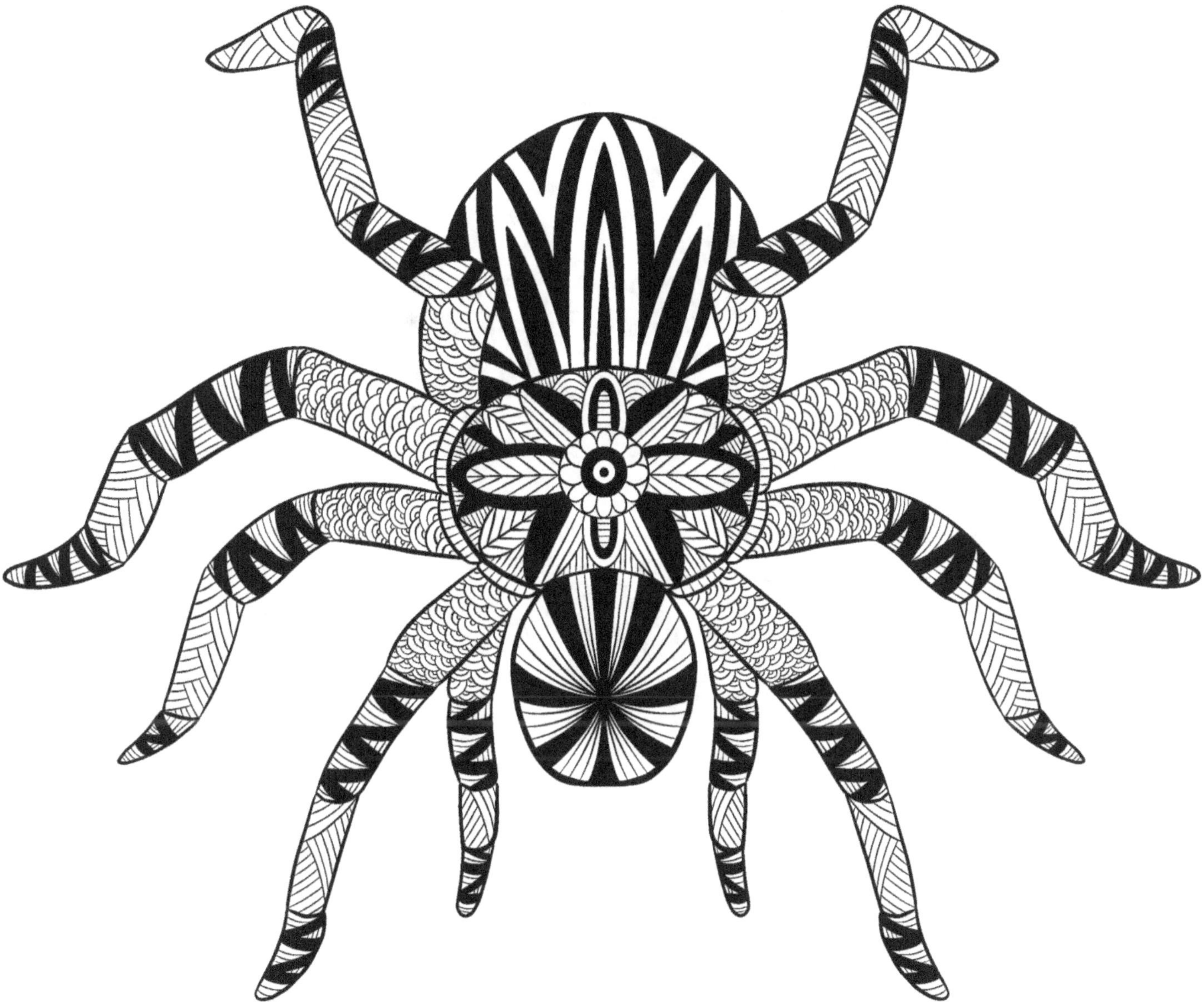

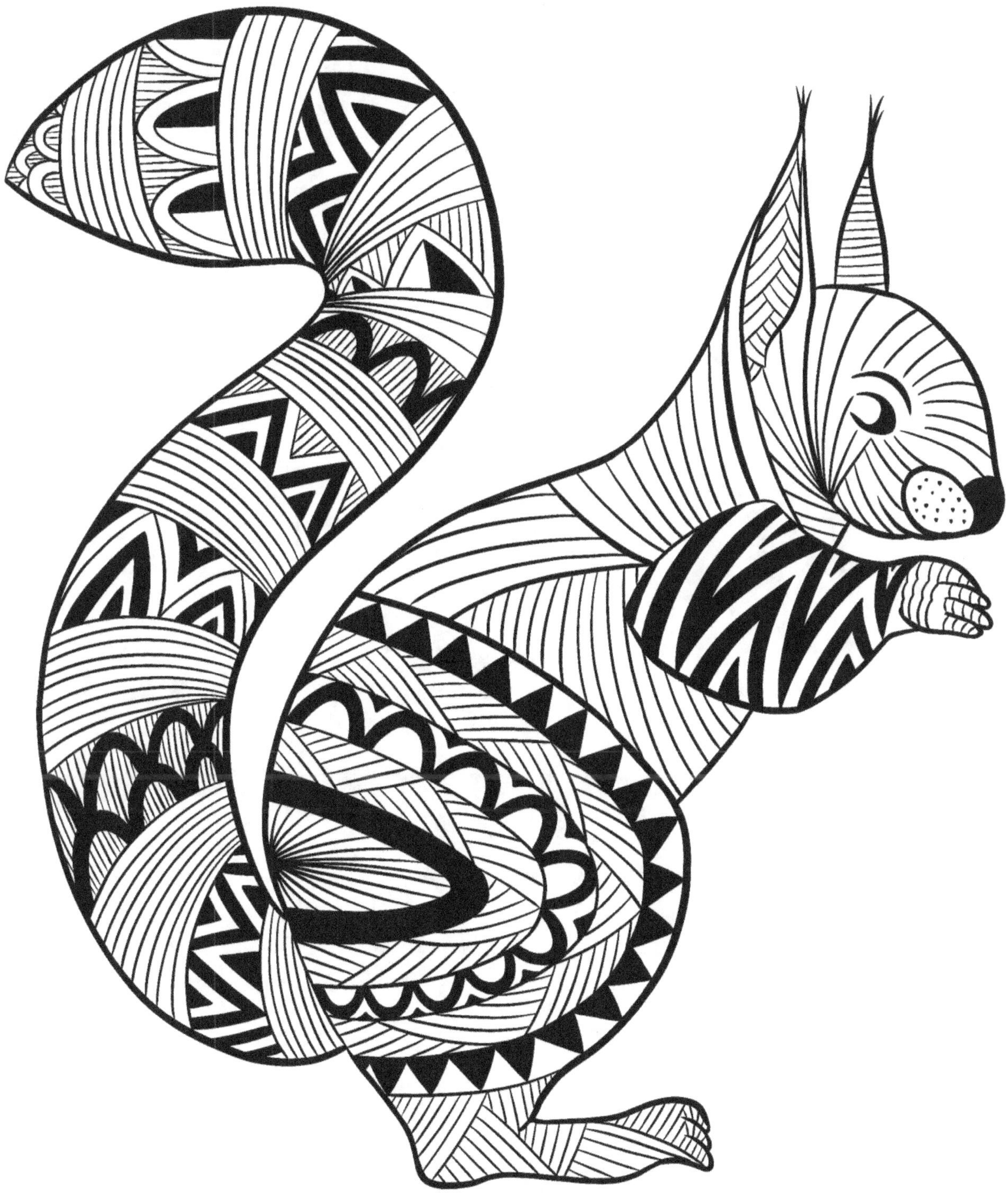

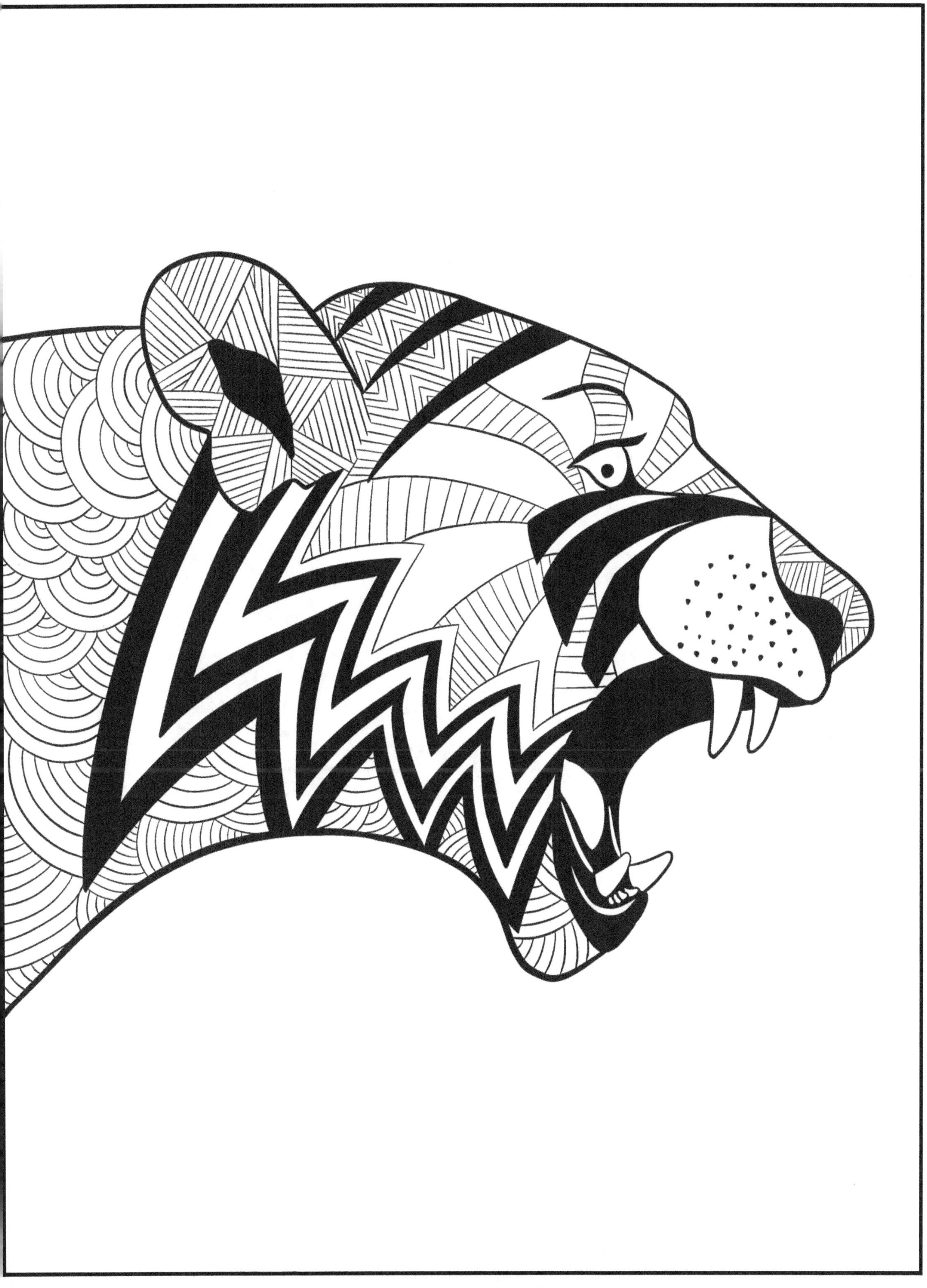

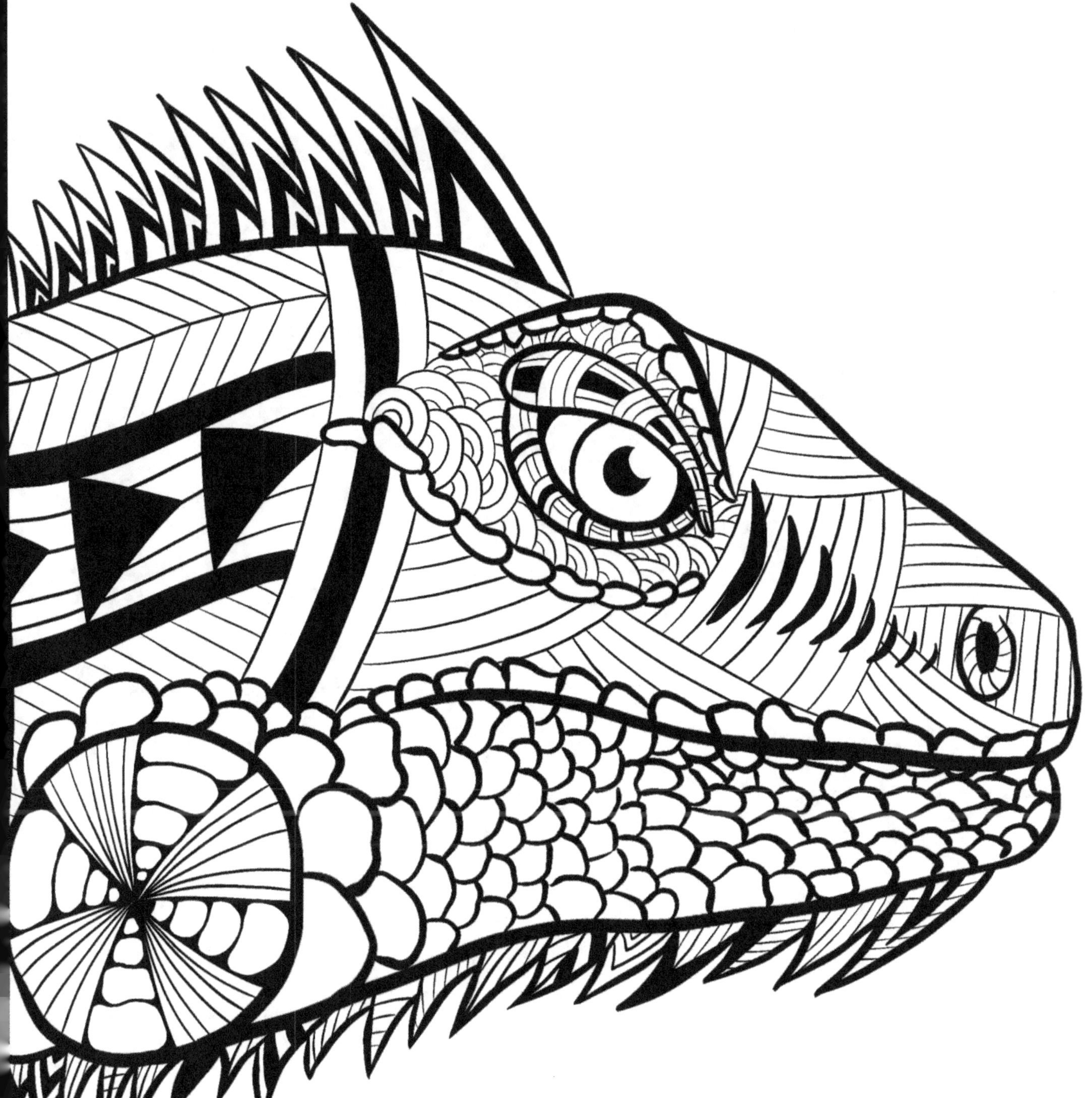

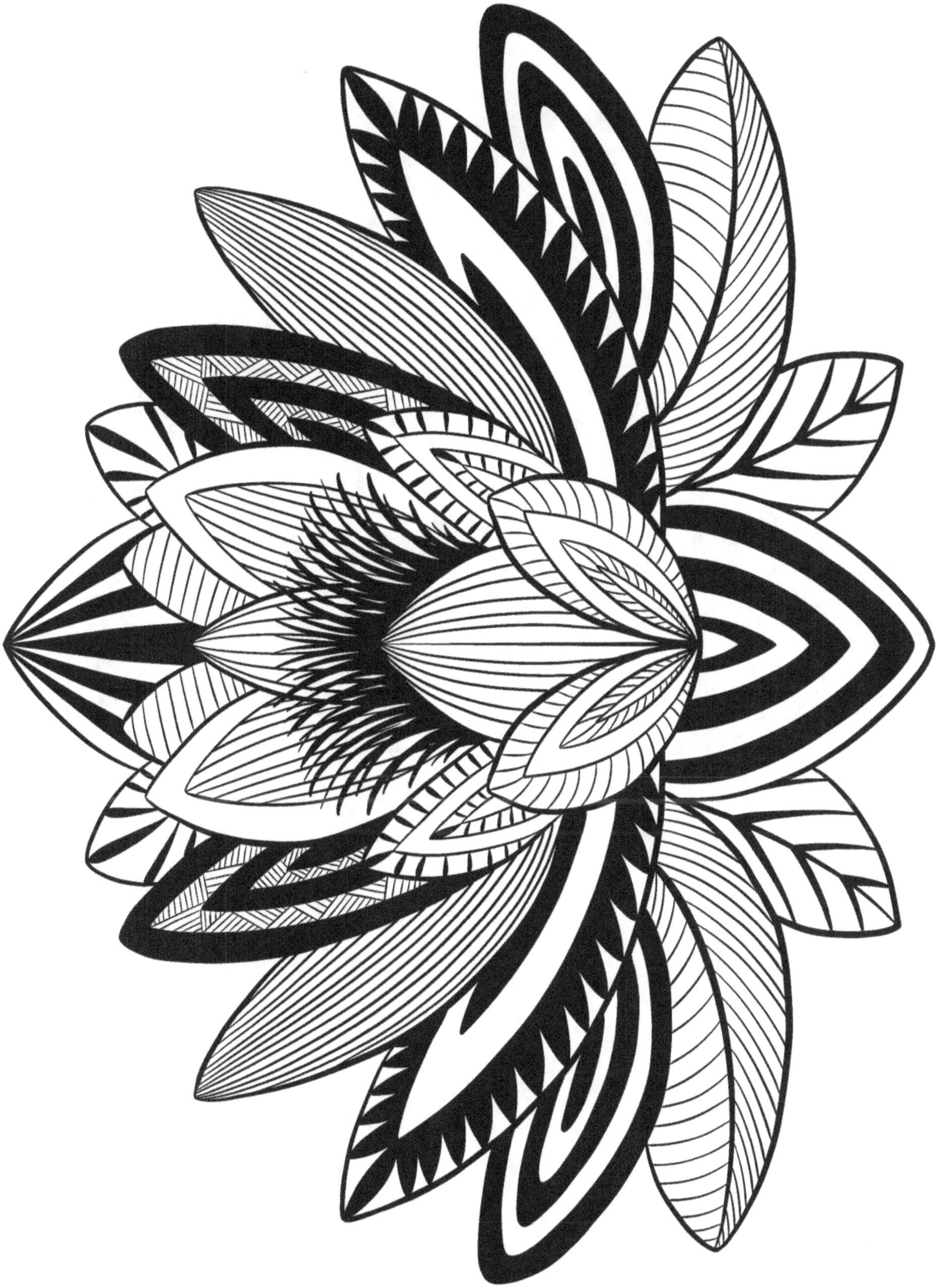

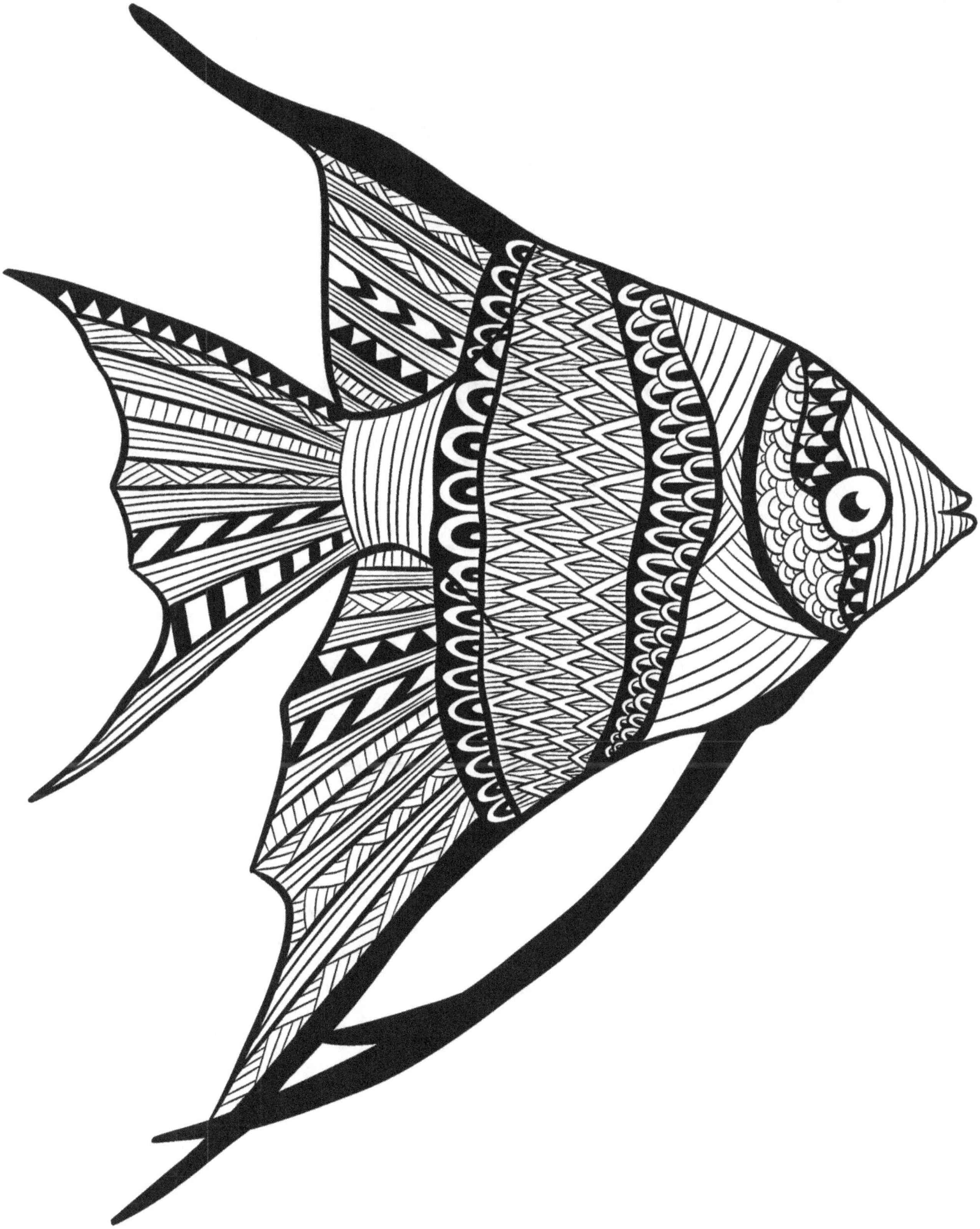

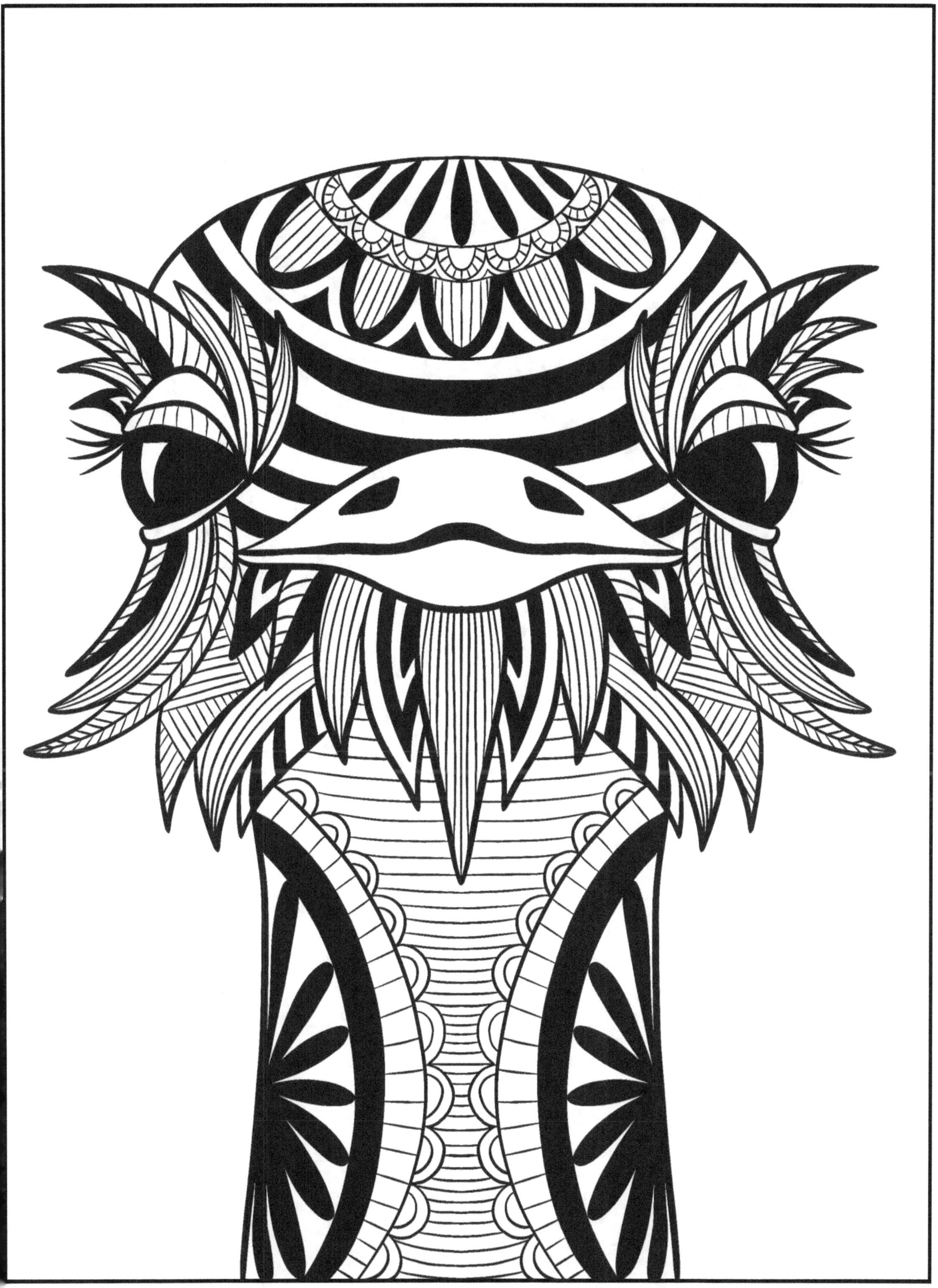

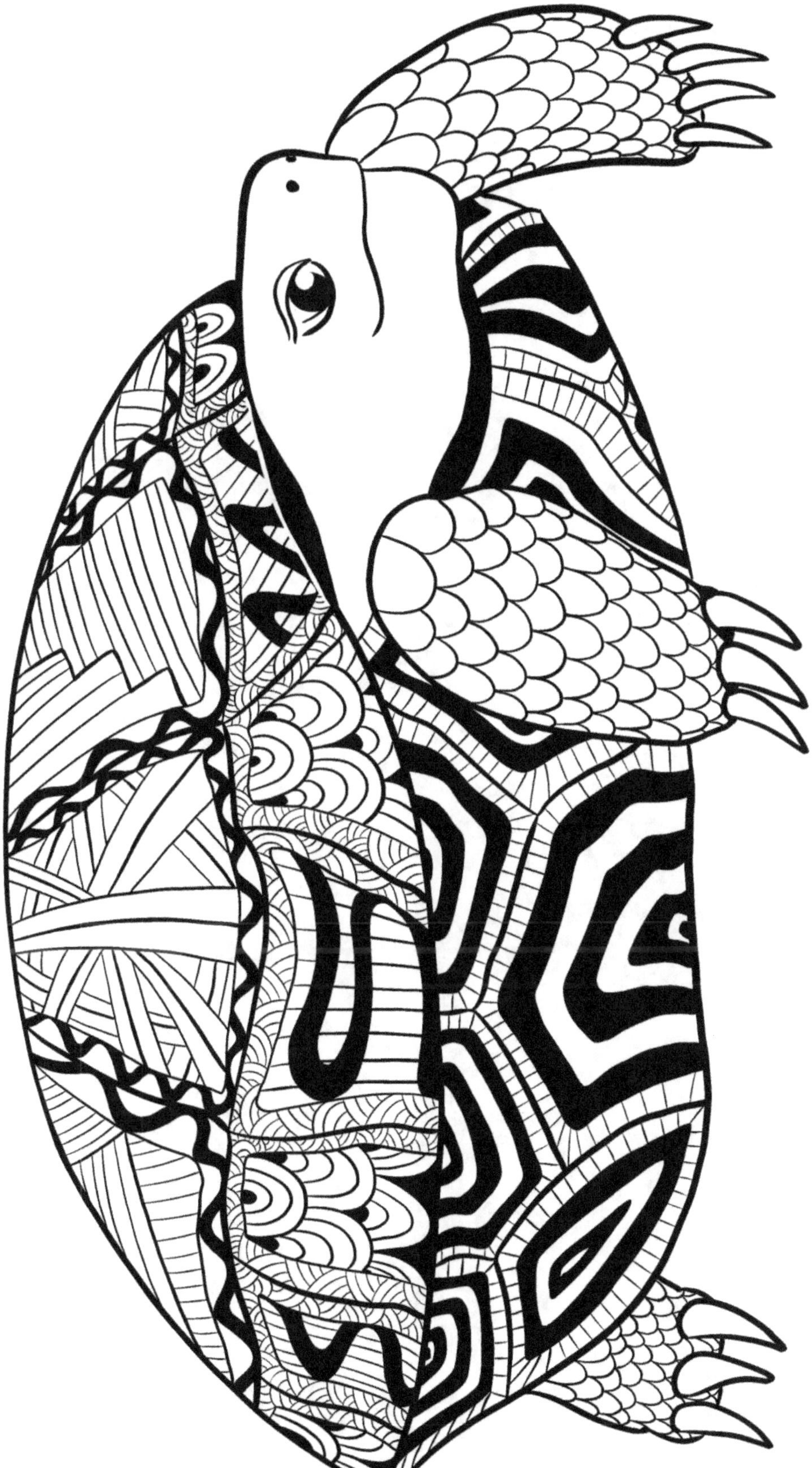

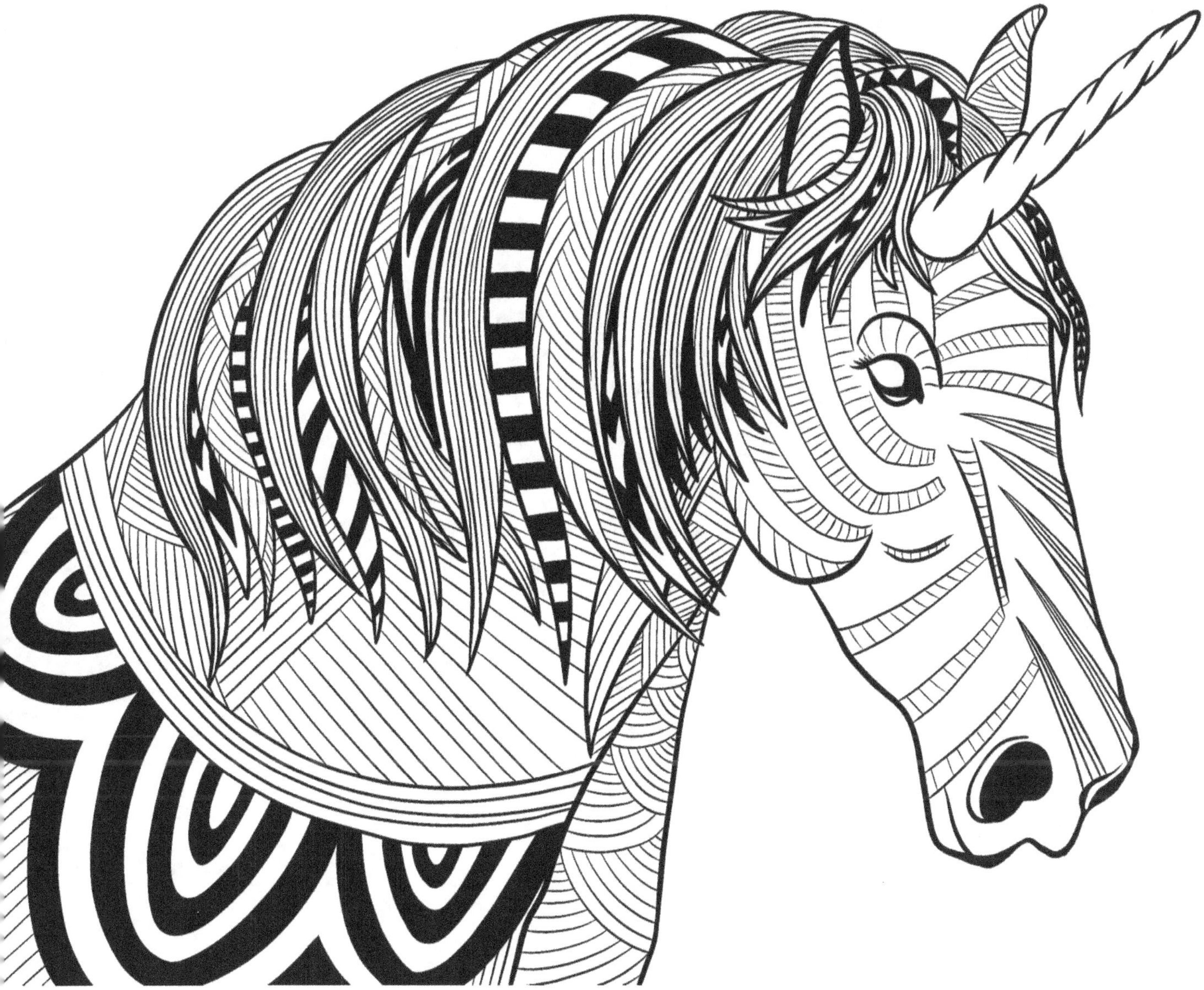

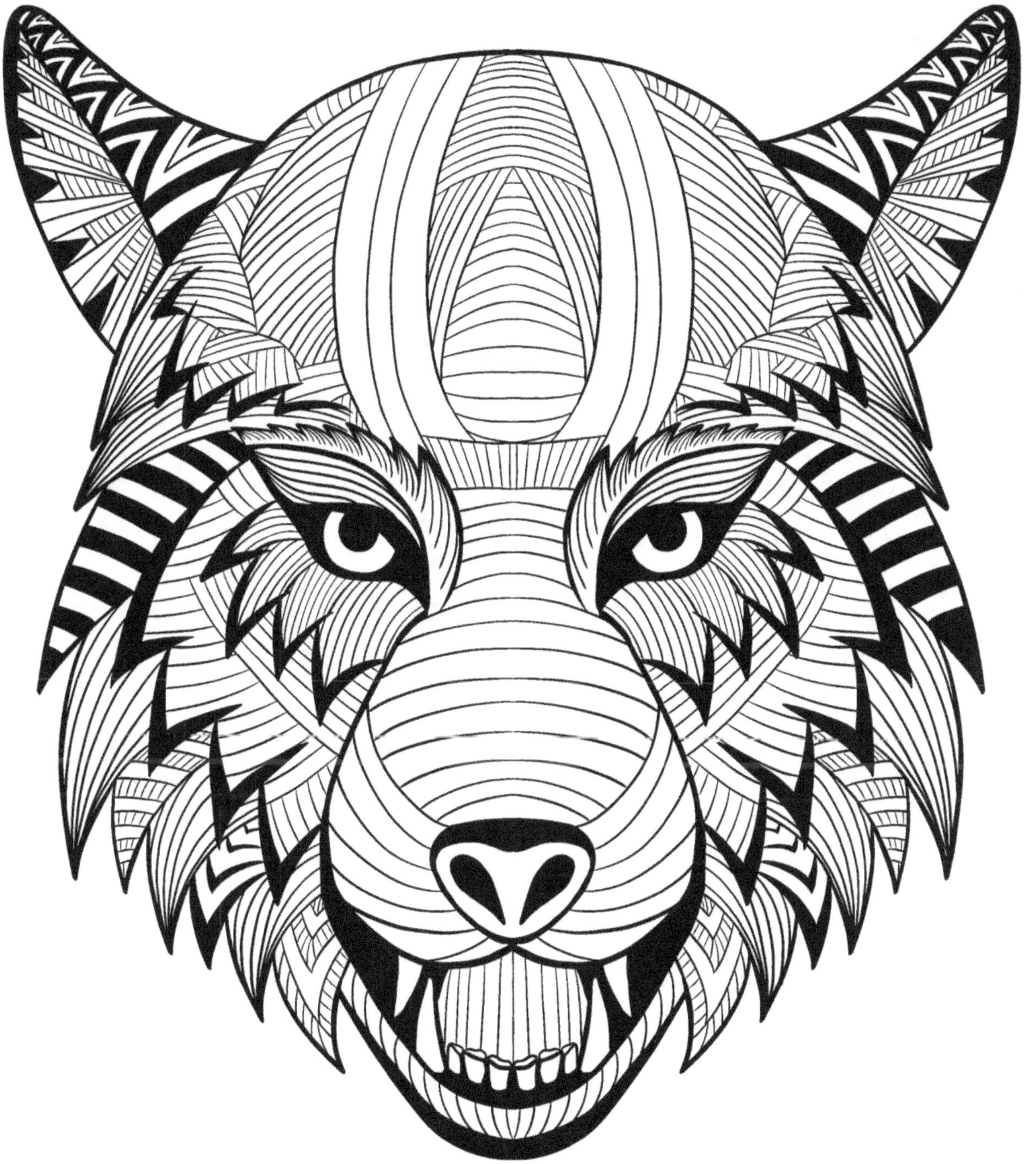

www.ingramcontent.com/pod-product-compliance
Lightning Source LLC
Chambersburg PA
CBHW080838220526
45467CB00008B/2312
9798716673823